STUART'S RECIPE
Book

Stuart Ralston

Catalogued Ideas and Random Thoughts

A Cookbook

Photography by Clair Irwin

Contents

6 Introduction
8 Scotland 1983–2006
11 Ingredients
14 Equipment

17 NYC
59 Aizle
125 Noto
177 Casual
221 Pickles and Chutneys
229 Oils and Emulsions
237 Breads

248 Index
254 Acknowledgements

Introduction

This is a cookbook, and it's also the story of me – of where I've come from and the places I've been. It's a snapshot of the things that have influenced me over the years and the people who've shaped me into who I am as a cook and, maybe more importantly, as a person.

I've always taken notes, and I've kept all my notebooks over the years – scrapbooks that I carry everywhere with me, where I scribble recipes, sketches for dishes, things I want to remember. I was always anxious I'd forget good ideas – I constantly have random thoughts about food, restaurants, dishes, staff, service ideas, layouts of possible restaurants – so they became a place to journal my life as I travelled, something to do when I was on my own in a coffee shop or dining by myself in a restaurant.

When I was in NYC I bought a book called *A Book of Ideas* by Aki Kamozawa and Alex Talbot. It was just a book with pictures, no recipes or info, with titles of dishes that were all very conceptual. I loved it. I looked up their blog, 'Ideas in Food', where they catalogued ideas and random thoughts and wrote them down in a list. I was massively inspired and started my own in 2008 – you can see some of it on the endpapers of this book. It's a never-ending document: some ideas worked, some are terrible, some I haven't made yet, some I never will, but I have always found it fascinating to go back to. Some ideas have stuck with me over twenty years and still feel relevant: this is truly when you start to realise what your style is, your personality as a chef.

When I started thinking about writing a book, I didn't want it to be just a chef's book of beautiful food that could only be created in a professional kitchen. I felt it should include all the food that has been important to me over the years – the food that's inspired me and the food that I like to eat, as well as favourites that I cook for my family at home. The menus at Aizle and Noto don't come from out of the blue, and my influences as a chef don't just come from the professional kitchens I have worked in. There's a humility in finding the beauty in all food, not just the higher end – after all that's what eating is about, enjoying the whole scale.

This book is divided into four main sections: NYC – where I was introduced into a whole new world as a chef and as a person; Aizle – the first restaurant I opened, where I see how far I can push myself in terms of standards, creativity and the craft of being a chef; Noto – my second restaurant, which is the type of place I think Edinburgh needs, delicious, busy, fun, refined food in a cool setting; and Casual – which has things I enjoy cooking for my wife and kids as well as dishes I grew up with, all just as important to me as my professional cookery.

Even if you're not a professional chef, you should be able to find inspiration for delicious food in any of those chapters. While the recipes in the Aizle chapter are technical and show you exactly how we put dishes together in the restaurant, you can always take elements of them to make a dinner at home – sirloin with cherry mustard for example, or wild turbot with vin blanc sauce and artichoke purée. There are some specialist ingredients and pieces of kit, but you can usually improvise when it comes to the equipment, and the ingredients are all easy to find on the internet. Either way, maybe this book will inspire you to try something new or push your own creative boundaries. I hope so.

Dickies

Scotland 1983–2006

I knew two things about myself from a very young age: I was going to become a chef and I wanted to explore the world beyond Scotland.

When I was nine, my family moved to Glenrothes, a tough, industrial town in Fife. It was an interesting place to grow up in the sense that there wasn't much to do, so we found things to do, which inevitably wound up with us getting into trouble.

I was lucky because my family knew how to eat and what it was to enjoy meals made from locally sourced ingredients. Not expensive dishes, but ones that used ingredients that were a challenge to prep. Now I realise how fortunate I was to experience that as a kid. It made me understand that great food is really about how you prepare it. Home-cooked food has always been my favourite and was normal for me growing up, but I realise that wasn't the case for every family in the UK.

My parents were both chefs. My dad loved all food, but his number one thing was always a 'true' pie – it had to have a bottom of pastry as well as a lid – and I distinctly remember being on holiday and my dad ripping into a waiter for the steak pie just having a lid of pastry. I always found it hilarious that he thought the temples of gastronomy resided at Butlins in Ayr.

My mum is Cornish and grew up in the fishing village of Newlyn. We had amazing summers there as kids and were always excited to visit. Some of my mum's family are fishermen and, in fact, my mum's family name, Kelynack, has a lot of history locally

Right: My mum with my older bother, Scott, and me. I'm in the middle.

Opposite: Ideas for adapting dishes recorded in great detail and never once cooked.

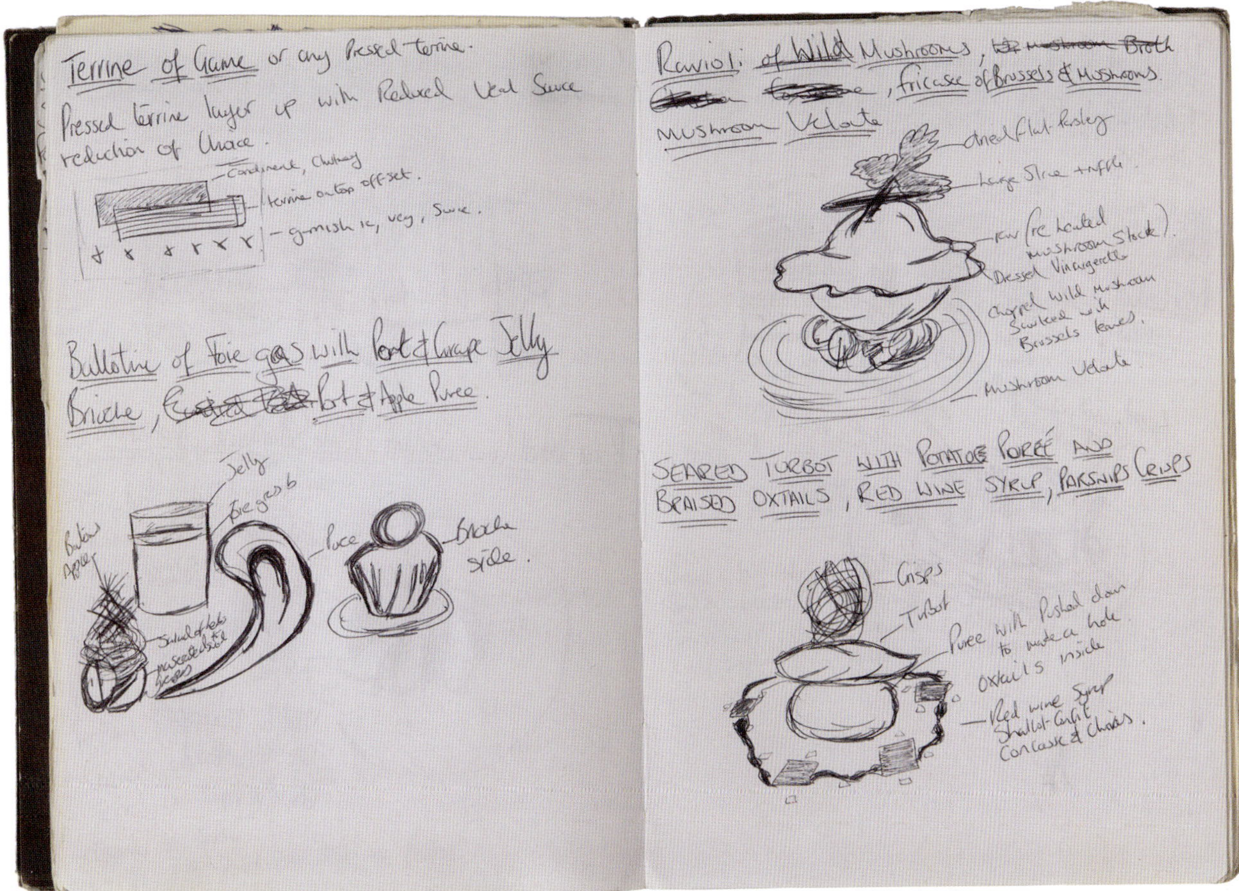

with Cornish fish markets. In 1851, Mary Kelynack is said to have walked from Cornwall to London with a turbot to give to the Queen. My mum's family didn't have a lot of money but always had access to plenty of fish! We'd eat amazing food when we were there, dressed crab, which we would make into sandwiches and eat at the beach, incredible saffron doughnuts and fresh ice cream from Jelbert's, topped with clotted cream.

After high school, I got a job working for a great chef at a small country hotel in Scotland. The chef was a formidable figure and he didn't talk much to me in the first three months, probably testing to see if I was worth his time. I learned the techniques of basic cookery there. Chef had a passion for fish, so we would get the best hand-dived scallops in the shell and use the roe for sauce-making, or prepare massive whole turbots for the starters.

I was 'live in' staff meaning I lived on-site, which at seventeen was a massive learning curve and, at times, very isolating. Living amongst other staff could be weird; there was a lot of waiting for the bathroom. Sharing the kitchen was interesting because many of the staff were from other European countries. I remember a French waiter who would make fresh coffee and a really wet omelette every morning before work. He didn't drink Nescafé? Strange…

It was a fairly typical kitchen. Everyone bantered about football and I learnt how to place horse racing bets for the sous chef and a lot of other life lessons. Chef hated laziness and had a disdain for anything other than a white and blue striped apron like the one worn by his hero Marco Pierre White. The general day-to-day here went: arrive around 9.30am, greet Chef and check how many covers you had booked. Chef was first in and would have written the menu and then you would make everyone a coffee and start to prep. By 11.30am it was staff lunch, which was usually either rolls or pies (staff nutrition wasn't a thing then). We would then get lunch under way, beginning with the canapés, followed by the starters and mains, tidy down, send desserts and sometimes get away for a 'split' (a break between 3 and 5pm before returning for dinner service). We would generally start serving the dinner tasting menu by

6pm, and once it was finished at around 9.30pm, we'd get cleaned down, empty the bins, clean the floors and finish for the day at 10.30pm. Even now I am not sure that everyone knows that a chef's day is a full day – morning and night we are at work.

Chef nurtured my already growing interest in international restaurants, sharing with me cookery books from all over the world. A lot of the books I own today Chef bought me, like *The French Laundry Cookbook*, where I saw Thomas Keller's game-changing American cuisine (probably the first real three-Michelin-starred chef that I had been exposed to). The book was so clean and fresh – it was clear he was on another level – and to me it was mind-blowing. Chef showed me Charlie Trotter's collection of books on meat and game, seafood and vegetables: I had never seen food like this before – it was modern but classic at the same time and the ingredients alone were completely different to anything I'd seen in Scotland. I was taken in by the mystique and mastery that Charlie Trotter exuded through the pages. He also bought me *Aquavit* by Marcus Samuelsson, the Ethiopian-born chef and owner of the Swedish restaurant of the same name in New York City. It was truly unique, ultra-modern, and the book's pictures and recipes were incredibly inspiring – this went on to become a very important book for me.

When I was 21, I moved on to a small luxury hotel not far from Edinburgh. The chef there was fantastic and had just returned to Scotland after time in England and France. He would frequently reminisce about his time in Paris working under Joël Robuchon: the hell he went through speaking no French and trying to get by with little money, no family or friends, all while being screamed at by an insane yet legendary three-Michelin-starred chef in a foreign tongue. It sounded like heaven. He was a great storyteller, and the tales of the ruthless kitchens of France really made me feel that my experiences so far had been inadequate. He ran a tough but fair kitchen. I remember an incident where the freezer hadn't been cleaned properly. He emptied it out on the floor and asked us why it was left in such a manner. Didn't we care about the food? Didn't we care about running a tight kitchen? I got his point; it seemed harsh but ultimately there was no room for these types of oversights if we wanted to emulate the great kitchens we had talked about. He used to mark up the Fairy Liquid so the KP could make it stretch the whole week, and he cut sponges in half so we wouldn't use as many. The food was great, but in some ways he was a greater influence on my business acumen than on my cooking.

I started to think seriously about working abroad, an idea that had crossed my mind before but that I had always swept aside as unrealistic. None of my family, friends, co-workers or anyone else I knew in my young life had left the UK to pursue a career in cooking. Hearing first-hand that it wasn't only possible, but realistic, made it tangible to me. The outside world wasn't so elusive after all.

I got busy. Since it had been a childhood dream of mine to live in New York City, I thought it was as good a place to start as any. I sent emails and filled in online applications for every two- and three-Michelin-starred kitchen in Manhattan and ended up receiving an offer for a week-long stage at Marcus Samuelsson's restaurant, Aquavit. I was euphoric: me holding a glossy cookbook in my hands in a tiny village in Scotland was about to become me standing in the Aquavit kitchen working alongside a lot of crazy talented young people.

Ingredients

We use some really special ingredients to create the food on our menus, and of course we have wonderful suppliers and the best fresh produce. But, especially at Aizle, ingredients can start to get complicated, and whilst you will find many of the items listed below in a professional kitchen, they aren't always available or even necessary at home. If you're curious, they're easy to find on the internet. This A–Z covers everything from the basics to the more unusual.

Agar Agar

We often use this for fluid gels. It's a plant-based setting agent, usually made from algae. It needs to be boiled to set as it has a much higher melting point than regular gelatine, which means you can make warm gelled items.

Algae Powder

We use algae powder to dye foods or to add a seafood flavour. It is a natural food colourant so saves us using too many chemical compounds.

Butter

Always use unsalted butter for cooking; this way you can control the salt content along the way. We make salted butter in-house for our bread service, using about 7% salt to preserve and season it.

Eggs

Always use free-range and always size large, and buy from the best source you can.

Fine Sea Salt

You will always need to adjust seasoning to your personal preference. My advice is to use a good quality fine sea salt, season from a height so you get even distribution and season gradually from the start, then cook a little and taste again throughout the process – this gives a better depth of flavour.

Fondant

We use commercial pouring fondant to glaze pastry items and when we're making caramels and tuiles and don't want the sugars to crystallise. It melts really easily.

Gelatine

Leaf gelatine comes in gold, silver and bronze grades. We always use gold leaf which has the highest amount of gelatine per sheet. You need to bloom it before you use it: soak the dried sheet in a bowl of cold water until it goes soft and jelly-like, then squeeze out the excess water and melt the leaf in whatever warm liquid you are setting. It will set once cold.

Glucose

A clear syrup that stops desserts and ice creams setting too firm, glucose can also be used for glazes.

Invert Sugar

Another commonly used sugar that is used to sweeten pastry items and slow down crystallisation in toffees, ice creams and sorbets, invert sugar can also help fresh goods to last longer. It's made from sugar, water and an acid (like cream of tartar, citric acid or even lemon juice), but you can buy it ready made.

Isomalt

This sugar substitute acts like a sweetener without using sugar – and incidentally it doesn't rot your teeth either. Commonly made from beetroots, we use it when we want something to crack like hardened sugar but we don't want too much sweetness.

Pomace Oil

Made from the leftovers of olive oil production, pomace oil is lower quality than olive oil but better than a plain vegetable oil. It has a neutral flavour so is ideal for dressings and infused oils.

Soy Lecithin

This is basically a fat stabiliser, which we mainly use in sauces such as a fish velouté. When you add it to a sauce then blend it with a hand blender, it creates that frothy cappuccino-style foam that people either love or hate.

Trisol

A soluble fibre derived from wheat, trisol gives things like batter a crispy texture and extra crunch.

Ultratex

This thickens a liquid into a gel, and it's really useful when working with smaller quantities. As you whisk the ultratex in, it takes just 2 to 3 minutes to thicken the liquid up.

Vegetable Oil

We only use this, the cheapest of oils, for searing meats and vegetables or roasting basic things. It has no flavour and a high burning point so it's good for browning foods and creating a Maillard reaction (the flavour development you need for things to taste good).

Vinegars

We use a ton of vinegars. I have a very high acid palette and I enjoy the refreshing burst vinegar brings to dishes and the way it elevates anything fatty. We use white wine vinegar for basic pickling and to clean our plates, and sherry vinegar to finish off roasted meats. We make wild leek vinegar in the spring and finish lamb sauces with it to replicate the vinegary mint sauce my mum used to make.

Xanthan Gum

This is very useful to emulsify or thicken things like vegetable purées: about 2% xanthan gum added to a purée when blending it at high speed will give it a much more silky feel and a smoother texture. It's easy to find online and in supermarkets in the free-from section.

Yeast

We use both fresh and dried yeast in the restaurants. Generally you'll need double the amount of fresh yeast than dried in any recipe. Fresh yeast goes off more quickly but it can be frozen, while dried yeast is really convenient for home use as it lasts a lot longer.

Sources

Google is your friend for any of the above, but here are some of the excellent suppliers we use for more niche ingredients.

waitrose.com
souschef.co.uk
sushisushi.co.uk
msk-ingredients.com
keylink.org
scotchfrost.com
westlandsuk.co.uk
de-burgh.com
alternativemeats.co.uk
marshpig.co.uk

Equipment

There are some bits of equipment that we use in the Aizle kitchen that you would be very unlikely to want or need at home. This is a run down of useful items as well as more obscure professional kit and suggestions for what you can use instead.

Cast Iron Pans

I'm a bit of a nerd when it comes to cast-iron pans. The thing about a cast-iron pan is that it will last forever: made from the hardest steels and forged at high temperatures, they hold the heat like no other pan, meaning you can cook things like steak at a constant high heat without a drop in cooking temperature. My pride and joy are my Griswold pans: they are collectors' items now, made by a company that started in America in 1865 and wound down in the late fifties. They do need a little love and care every couple of months, but if they're looked after they retain a non-stick layer and never rust.

Croustade Iron

This is an old-school bit of French kit to make canapé shells: you heat it up in oil, then dip it into whatever batter you're using, then back into the hot oil. The batter cooks and then slips off the iron into the hot oil, meaning you get exactly the same shape of shell each time.

Dehydrator

This is a handy piece of equipment that helps us keep things dry and crispy. We also use a dehydrator to dry purées into glass-like sheets.

Gram Scale

As a rule, I measure everything by weight rather than volume for precision and consistency. It cuts down on time and the need to use various measuring tools, so a gram scale really makes things easier. It annoys me when a cookbook goes from gram weights to teaspoons to millilitres, so nearly everything in here is measured in weight. Digital scales are pretty cheap and last well, and it's useful to have accurate gram scales for weighing small amounts of ingredients like spices or agar agar.

Hand Blender

Also known as stick blenders, hand blenders are great for blending small quantities of gels and spices. We also use them to emulsify chocolate ganache or to aerate sauces like fish velouté. Get a powerful one like a Bamix.

iSi Siphon Gun

These pressurised cream whipper guns allow you to add nitrous oxide directly into a liquid, instantly giving you a light and airy texture.

Japanese Mandolin

A mandolin is used to slice vegetables uniformly wafer thin: it's basically a narrow board with a super sharp blade in the middle. It does cut down on knife work but use it with caution: I've seen many a cut in the kitchens from these.

Kilner Jars
We mainly use Kilner jars for keeping pickles, preserves and fermentations, but they're just generally great for storage. The air-tight seal keeps the contents free from oxygen so they last longer, and they're really good for storing sourdough starters.

Liquid Nitrogen
A super cool thing to play around with but one that needs to be used very carefully, liquid nitrogen is a very cold liquid that sits at -195°C. This means we can deep-freeze things instantly and create different textures and edible snow-like powders that would be impossible to achieve in a regular freezer.

Microplane
This is really useful to zest lemons, shave cheese and grate garlic.

Moulds
We have a huge collection (humble brag) of different shapes and sizes of non-stick Teflon moulds for pastry cases and silicone moulds for frozen desserts, mousses and chocolates. If I've mentioned an unusual shape or size in a recipe, there will also be an alternative.

Oven Temperatures
We use Rational ovens at the restaurants, which combine convection and steam to cook food evenly and are very accurate. The oven temperatures in these recipes are for fan assisted ovens.

Pasta Machine
Invaluable if you ever want to make your own pasta: it is almost impossible to roll out pasta as efficiently or consistently by hand. We also use ours to make thin crisps like the lavosh crackers on page 111.

Pizza Oven
This one's a luxury item for sure, but pizza ovens are becoming more common in home gardens. I have a Gozney Roccbox and it beats takeaway pizza hands down. You can replicate a similar feel by cooking your pizza in a hot, heavy cast-iron pan, then finishing it in a regular oven – it holds the heat much better.

Plastic Piping Bags
Plastic ones are best: they can be cleaned and reused; they don't absorb flavours, smells or colours like cloth pastry bags; and they are very versatile when it comes to using tips as you can cut them to any size.

Smoker Gun
A battery-operated smoker gun is pretty easy to use: just turn it on, place a small amount of wood chips in the gun's chamber and light with a flame. An integral fan pushes the cool smoke down a hose to wherever you want it, smoking small items in minutes. We use it for all sorts of things, from vegetables to dairy items like cheese or creams.

Spiraliser
Another good tool to cut down on knife work and get consistent results, a spiraliser creates spaghetti-type shapes from vegetables and gives a different texture to everything from potato to radish.

Steamer
A simple bamboo steamer with a lid is inexpensive and accessible and very handy to keep at home. We use a commercial steamer in the restaurant for things like custards, but at home I use bamboo ones for dumplings and fish.

Thermometers
We use two different kinds of thermometers: digital thermometers to take temperatures of everything from cooked meats to the water that goes into breads, and sugar thermometers to measure how hot caramels are as they have very specific temps for soft or harder cracks.

Thermomix
We use our Thermomixes all day long. A Thermomix is a very powerful blender that can also weigh ingredients and be programmed to cook things: they get purées silky smooth and are great for making things like custards without using a pan. They are also extremely expensive, but in most circumstances a good upright blender will do a similar job.

NYC

The city that has had the biggest impact on me is New York City, which might seem strange seeing as I'm from a small town in Scotland. Moving to New York to work for Gordon Ramsay was the single biggest turning point in my life and presented me with opportunities I would never have had at home. It made me a better chef by far, but more importantly it made me grow up as a person: the exposure to so many different cultures and cuisines; working with people from all over the world; living in a truly global city. I met my wife, Krystal, in New York; it's where we got our first apartment together, and we shared many meals all over the city. This a collection of our favourite things to eat from that time, a mix of high-end and casual dishes with flavours that influence how I cook in my own restaurants now.

New York City
2006–2011

I won't lie, New York City was intimidating. It felt very surreal from the moment I touched down. The sheer enormity of the buildings, the noise from the traffic, the constant honking of car horns and the incessant sirens all gave me heart palpitations. It was night-time and the whole city was lit up – it is constantly lit up, but at night it really comes to life and you can see the mist in the sky because of the lights.

I had flown there by myself and booked into a hotel. I had no idea how to use the subway, get food for myself or even confidently order a coffee which all sounds ridiculous now. The experience was terrifying. I had never been completely on my own and never thought of myself as unconfident but NYC brought that all out in spades.

During the week at Aquavit I kept my head down, stayed quiet, did what I was asked and observed a lot. They all wore baseball caps as part of their uniforms, not like UK kitchens where skull caps are mandatory. I watched food I had no idea how to cook be plated. It was almost like I didn't even know what cooking was, the style was so different and new to me. I didn't feel confident even trying to jump in and talk about it, and it was BUSY, like over 100 people a service. A couple of dishes really stuck with me, including the pickled herring that came with a Carlsberg (of all beers!) and a shot of house aquavit. There was also the hot foie gras ganache with duck pastrami, cherry chutney and whipped goat's cheese which required such delicacy to unmould; imagine a foie gras version of a hot chocolate fondant and that was it.

The flight home was a mental struggle. On the one hand, I was certain that I couldn't return to New York: it was too much for someone like me to handle, it was expensive, and everything was so foreign to me it almost felt threatening. But by the time I picked up my luggage at baggage claim, I knew that Scotland had taught me all it could and that I had to follow my ambitions by returning to New York City and finishing what I had started.

Right: Taken at the airport in 2006 when I left for New York; it was the last time I saw my dad.

Opposite: Some of my more detailed doodles with ideas for plating.

When I got home, I wrote to my idol, Gordon Ramsay himself, asking for a job at his soon-to-open NYC outpost at The London. I soon heard that there was the possibility of a position but I would have to complete a trial at The Connaught in London. I went down, and after I'd checked in to the kitchen, I was given a list of 'basic jobs' to complete: *Brunoise shallot. Mayonnaise. Blanch green beans. Turn artichoke. Lemon vinaigrette. Fillet a bream. Bone and cook lamb saddle (mi saignant).* This list had me in bounds of stress. It was a test of basic cookery skills but somehow turning an artichoke just hadn't come up before now, and I had never made a mayonnaise from scratch or learnt how to blanch green beans. I fumbled around the jobs, realising the gaps in my training and feeling inadequate again. A Scottish sous chef told me to take my time, that they wanted to see if I could do things properly, that I should use only salt to season my meat and fish as they hated black pepper, and that the French word, *saignant*, which I had no fucking clue about, meant medium-rare. It was a life raft and when I thought I had done enough I called Chef over to check my work. My brunoise was too chunky, my mayonnaise wasn't silky smooth but greasy and half split, the green beans weren't cooked enough and I'd under-salted the cooking water, and the artichoke had turned brown. Chef was kind enough not to berate me, though I knew my trial had not been up to standard.

So I can hardly describe the sheer joy I felt when a few weeks later I received an offer to be part of the opening team for Gordon Ramsay at the London NYC. I thought I had messed the whole thing up, but Chef had seen something of value in me. I never asked any of the usual job questions like *When do I start?* or *How much does it pay?* because none of that mattered – I was going to live in New York City. I was 23 years old and going to work for Gordon Ramsay. They could have offered to pay me in monkey nut shells and I would have agreed just as eagerly. This was it.

Before my arrival in New York I'd tried every single avenue to rent a room or an apartment with no success, so I'd booked into a hotel. This was in fact a cunningly disguised and well-marketed dive of a hostel that largely housed the homeless, domestic abuse victims and those with addiction issues. There was a shared bathroom, lots of mailboxes and a lot of hard, worn-looking. Nevertheless, it was cheap. I had the unfortunate experience of listening to people argue and fight during the day before saying goodnight to them in the shared bathroom as we brushed our teeth before bed.

Despite living in a shit-hole and running out of money, I had an energy and appetite like no other for this experience. I felt very positive – perhaps completely in denial about how hard things were about to get – and I relished it all. I just wanted to get into the kitchen, get over the formalities, start the process and get the nerves out of the way. I was living on a $1.09 cup of coffee from Starbucks in the morning and a giant $2 slice of cheese pizza on the way back to the hostel. Good living for just $3.09 a day!

I spent every day walking to the restaurant, just to make sure I knew how to get there on foot and how long it took. From the shitty hostel it was a 45-minute walk but I was still intimidated by the subway, plus it was another expense I couldn't afford. I walked by the front of the restaurant every day, past a giant Ramsay poster – a familiar face and a reminder of why I was there. I walked every day, every night, everywhere. On the last night before I was due to start, Gordon Ramsay himself passed me in the street. He obviously had no idea who I was, but to see my idol casually walking by, the person I had turned my life upside down for, was surreal. This god-like figure in my head was a normally dressed person, very tall, wearing a black leather jacket and a white t shirt.

The standards at The London were so much higher than I had known. The attention to detail had been dialled up by about 200%. Every single item was inspected by a senior chef, every purée was tasted, your uniform had to be sharp, you had to have shaved every day. I remember prepping ten trays of tomato 'petals' – the skins had to be removed and the slices laid in trays, then each petal got a single sliver of garlic and a leaf of thyme. In other kitchens, a general sprinkling everywhere would have done the trick; here every single piece counted.

I had imagined myself in the Gordon Ramsay restaurant surrounded by polished plates and gleaming stoves, preparing beautiful food in highly focused surroundings. The reality was that as a commis on the veg I was kept downstairs in the prep rooms churning out turned artichokes by the case,

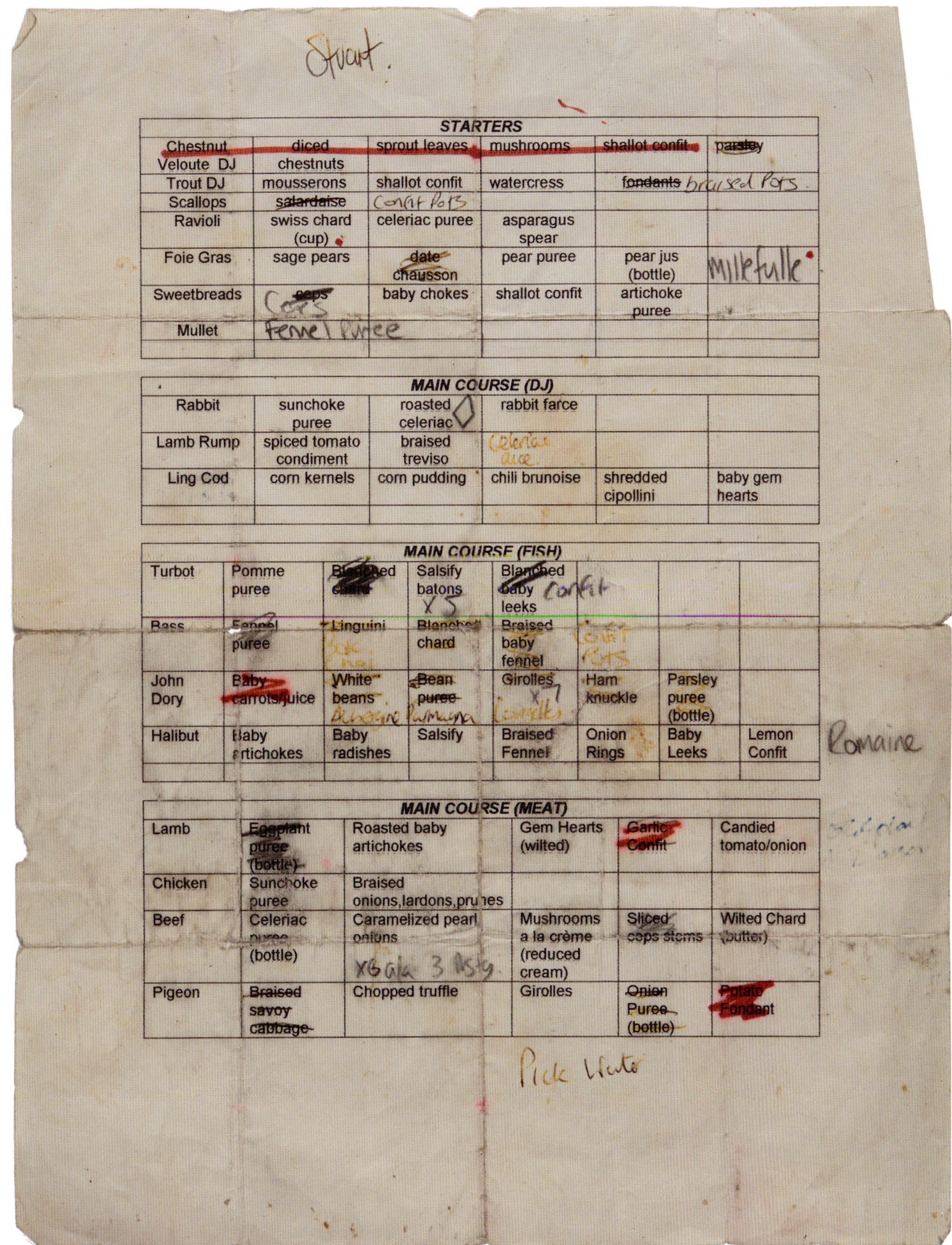

Stuart.

STARTERS					
Chestnut Veloute DJ	diced chestnuts	sprout leaves	mushrooms	shallot confit	parsley
Trout DJ	mousserons	shallot confit	watercress	fondants braised Pots	
Scallops	salardaise	Confit Pots			
Ravioli	swiss chard (cup)	celeriac puree	asparagus spear		
Foie Gras	sage pears	date chausson	pear puree	pear jus (bottle)	Millefulle
Sweetbreads	ceps Ceps	baby chokes	shallot confit	artichoke puree	
Mullet	Fennel Puree				

MAIN COURSE (DJ)					
Rabbit	sunchoke puree	roasted celeriac	rabbit farce		
Lamb Rump	spiced tomato condiment	braised treviso	Celeriac dice		
Ling Cod	corn kernels	corn pudding	chili brunoise	shredded cipollini	baby gem hearts

MAIN COURSE (FISH)							
Turbot	Pomme puree	Blanched chard	Salsify batons x5	Blanched baby leeks Confit			
Bass	Fennel puree	Linguini Bok Choi	Blanched chard	Braised baby fennel	Confit Pots		
John Dory	Baby carrots/juice	White beans	Bean puree	Girolles x7	Ham knuckle	Parsley puree (bottle)	
Halibut	Baby artichokes	Baby radishes	Salsify	Braised Fennel	Onion Rings	Baby Leeks	Lemon Confit

Romaine

MAIN COURSE (MEAT)					
Lamb	Eggplant puree (bottle)	Roasted baby artichokes	Gem Hearts (wilted)	Garlic Confit	Candied tomato/onion
Chicken	Sunchoke puree	Braised onions,lardons,prunes			
Beef	Celeriac puree (bottle)	Caramelized pearl onions	Mushrooms a la crème (reduced cream)	Sliced ceps stems	Wilted Chard (butter)
Pigeon	Braised savoy cabbage	Chopped truffle	Girolles	Onion Puree (bottle)	Potato Fondant

Pick Water

Above: The list of veg I had to have ready daily when working on the prep section at Gordon Ramsay.

preparing concasséd tomatoes by the kilo and peeling grelot onions non-stop. The realisation that it was going to be a very long time before I got even anywhere near the main kitchen was disappointing, but it did give me time to hone my skills, observe the upstairs teams and work out what it would take for me to get up there full-time.

After a couple of months, you started to see people either getting fired or just walking out and never coming back. The pressure was immense, the hours were tough and the high standards felt so hard to achieve. I could see why so many failed to be successful there. But with all the departures, I managed to get into the main kitchen and start on one of the sections. Every time someone left, you got to move on to the next section, so I started on garnish and then a few months later someone was leaving on fish and I would be eyeing up that spot. I used to be so nervous at the start of service on a new section that sometimes I'd actually be sick. I didn't tell anyone, I'd just run out the back quickly before 5pm and throw up in the giant bins.

I remember a service where the pressure and stress were at an all-time high and things just weren't clicking into place. I was on garnish and another chef was on fish. I had to make a sweetcorn risotto and the fish chef was going on a lobster ravioli. Somewhere the communication wasn't clear between us, and after the five-minute countdown I put up the risotto and the lobster ravioli wasn't in. Fucking disaster. I remember the chef being well and truly fucked off, like all the disappointments in the world had all come at him at once, and he just flipped; he threw the risotto down on the stove in anger and it flew up and hit me on the chest, spilling some on my neck and hands. He just couldn't contain the frustration of things not coming together. I was fine – mortified, but fine – and I cleaned up with just a couple of little burns. It really highlighted the pressure that people are under in these kitchens – the importance of timings, the attention to the minutest details and ultimately how seriously people take the job. I wasn't even angry with the chef; I just felt bad for him. I knew how much he was putting in.

Often after the dinner service at Gordon Ramsay we'd all go on a night out and end up eating somewhere. Blue Ribbon on Sullivan Street in Soho opened from 4pm to 4am and was a great place to hang out for drinks but also food – they had an amazing raw bar, fried chicken, steak tartar, fried oysters and the signature beef marrow roasted with oxtail marmalade. We had the best times there and that was the kind of place I was trying to create thirteen years later with Noto.

Right: My official work card for NYC. I probably could have smiled but the immigration people were slightly off-putting.

ONE WAY
BIKE LANE
TD Bank

Aquavit

The first kitchen I stepped into in NYC was Aquavit, the amazing Swedish-inspired restaurant from Marcus Samuelsson. One thing that really stood out was the massive vats of homemade aquavit they had. I'd never heard of it before I left Scotland, but I fell in love with it immediately. I like drinking it instead of gin with tonic and ice, but it's also great used in cocktails or drunk as a shot.

Makes 1 litre

5g coriander seeds
2.5g black pepper
7g cardamom pods
0.5g cloves
1g fennel seeds
2g caraway seeds

10g dill
peel of 2 limes
peel of 1 orange
peel of 1 lemon

1 litre Absolut vodka

In a dry frying pan, toast the coriander, black pepper, cardamom, cloves, fennel and caraway until a light smoke comes from the pan and the seeds crackle.

Put the toasted seeds, dill and citrus peel into a large jar, then pour over the vodka. Alternatively, pour about 50ml out of the vodka bottle and stuff everything straight in. Close the lid and leave to infuse for 2 days before drinking.

Pizza

When I first arrived in NYC, pizza by the slice was a godsend. At the time you could get a slice of cheese pizza for $2 from the chain 2 Bros, so living became cheap. Don't get me wrong – there's way better pizza to be had, and after I'd lived there a while my favourite was probably from Roberta's in Williamsburg, but I loved that pizza slice and I still have to eat one when I visit the city.

Now homemade pizza is probably my sons' favourite dinner. I cook them in my garden on a Gozney Roccbox – the best. I don't like too many wacky ingredients: just a good tomato sauce, mushrooms and cheese, or a little prosciutto laid on top after the pizza is cooked. Use fior de latte if you can find it; it's not as wet as most mozzarella so it won't make your pizza soggy.

Serves 4–6

4 balls Pizza Dough (recipe follows)

1 recipe San Marzano Tomato Sauce (recipe follows)
250g fior de latte, drained
120g chestnut mushrooms, thinly sliced

10–12g basil leaves

Preheat the oven to 220°C and line four large baking trays with parchment paper.

On a well-floured surface, press one ball of dough into a disc shape, and then begin to stretch the dough thinner and wider, keeping the surface well floured. Stretch to a 25cm circle and carefully transfer to one of the prepared baking trays.

Spread the base with tomato sauce, then tear pieces of fior de latte on top. Cover generously with sliced chestnut mushrooms.

Bake in the oven for 3 minutes, then rotate the tray and continue to cook until the base is nicely browned, approximately 2 to 3 minutes more. Once cooked, scatter over a few basil leaves, transfer to a cutting board and serve immediately.

Repeat with the remaining ingredients, baking one pizza at a time and taking care to allow the oven to get back up to temperature before baking each one.

Recipes continue on page 28

Pizza Dough

Makes 4 balls

300g strong white bread flour
300g 00 pasta flour
6g dry active yeast
400g warm water
15g salt
10g olive oil

In a stand mixer with dough hook attachment, mix the bread flour, pasta flour, yeast, water, salt and olive oil until a smooth elastic ball is formed, about 10 minutes.

Take the dough out of the bowl and rest on a table for 10 minutes under a damp cloth. Once rested, knock the air out, then shape it into a nice tight ball. Place the dough in a bowl and cover tightly with clingfilm.

Leave the dough to prove in a warm place for 2 to 3 hours until it has doubled in size, or put it straight in the fridge for 18 to 24 hours. If you've put the dough in the fridge, take it out 45 minutes before you want to make pizza to let it come to room temperature.

Tip the dough onto a floured worktop and cut into four equal-sized pieces, then shape each one into a ball.

San Marzano Tomato Sauce

Makes 500g

800g tinned San Marzano tomatoes

4 cloves garlic, finely chopped
salt

In a colander, leave the tomatoes to drain for 10 minutes, then blend them with the garlic and salt.

Roberta's

Banh Mi

My love for Japanese, Korean and Vietnamese flavours really came about in New York. A cook at Gordon Ramsay told me about a banh mi place called Saigon Bakery, located in the back of a jewellery shop on Grand Street. After stumbling in, thinking you're in the wrong place because it's filled with gold chains, you get to the counter at the back and place your order. It was cash only, and from memory the banh mi were huge – easily enough for two people, or for me to eat half for lunch and half for dinner. They cost maybe $7 back in 2006 – inexpensive but absolute class. You want to use a soft-ish baguette or the fillings fall out when you eat it.

Serves 1–2

1 fresh French baguette
50g shop-bought chicken liver paté
2 pieces Char Sui Chicken (recipe follows)
50g cucumber, cut into sticks
1 recipe Brined Vegetables (recipe follows)
½ recipe Kewpie Mayo (page 233)
3–4 red chillies, sliced
10g fresh coriander

Preheat your oven to 200°C and put the baguette in to warm for 10 minutes. Once warm, slice it in half horizontally and spread one side with chicken liver paté.

Slice up the char sui chicken into thin slithers and layer on top of the paté. Add the cucumber and some brined vegetables, then top with kewpie mayo, chillies and plenty of fresh coriander. Put the other half of the baguette on top and squeeze closed.

Recipes continue on page 32

Char Sui Chicken

Serves 4

50g tamari soy
50g hoisin sauce
50g runny honey
30g tomato ketchup
10g toasted sesame oil
3g Chinese five spice
3 garlic cloves, finely chopped
2–3 dashes Maggi liquid seasoning
Sriracha hot sauce

8 boneless, skinless chicken thighs

Preheat the oven to 210°C.

In a large bowl, mix together the tamari, hoisin, honey, ketchup, sesame oil, five spice, garlic and Maggi seasoning. Add a dash or two of Sriracha to taste, then stir in the chicken thighs and make sure they're well coated.

Place the chicken on a tray lined with tin foil and parchment paper. Roast in the oven for 20 minutes, then rest for another 10 minutes.

Brined Vegetables

Makes 200g

You will have enough for two or three sandwiches so keep any you don't eat in the brine for another time.

100g carrot
100g firm daikon radish
10g sugar
5g salt

Peel the carrot and daikon and then chop into longish sticks and put them in a bowl. Add the sugar and salt and massage them into the vegetables. Set aside for 20 minutes, until you start to see some brine gather, then wash the carrot and daikon off and dry on kitchen towel.

Astoria Gyro

Astoria is a neighbourhood in Queens hailed for its diverse cultural makeup, including a well-established Greek community. My wife Krystal and I had our first place together there, a classic New York apartment with the fire escape on the side. We loved it; we were super happy and having a great time (apart from the time we got bed bugs and they took over the whole apartment). Anyway, after work I would catch the NQRW line back to Astoria; I'd get off at Broadway and get a gyro from one of the stands outside the train station to eat on the way home – super cheap and so good.

Serves 4

4 Flatbreads (page 239), warmed
90g Hummus (recipe follows)
1 round butter lettuce

1 recipe Chicken Souvlaki (recipe follows)

80g Cucumber and Yoghurt Chutney (page 205)
2 large tomatoes, chopped
1 red onion, chopped

Spread each warmed flatbread with a generous slathering of hummus, then lay a few whole lettuce leaves on top.

Thinly slice the chicken straight off the skewers – like a shawarma – and layer onto the lettuce.

Top with a decent spoonful of cucumber and yoghurt chutney, some chopped tomatoes and onions, then wrap it all up.

Recipes continue on page 34

Hummus

Makes about 270g

1 × 400g tin chickpeas, drained
100g olive oil
30g tahini
2 garlic cloves
3g cumin powder
zest and juice of ½ lemon
3g salt

Blend the chickpeas, olive oil, tahini, garlic, cumin, lemon zest and juice and salt in a food processor or blender until smooth. Season with additional salt and lemon juice as needed. Store in an airtight container in the fridge for up to a week.

Chicken Souvlaki

Serves 4

10 boneless, skinless chicken thighs

10g smoked paprika
5g ground cumin
5g ground garlic powder
5g ground coriander
3g ground cinnamon
5g fresh oregano, chopped
5g fresh mint, chopped
5g fresh dill, chopped
8 garlic cloves, peeled and roughly chopped
90g good olive oil

1 large onion, halved

4 × 20cm metal or bamboo skewers (soak in cold water overnight to stop them burning)

Cut each chicken thigh into four.

In a large bowl, mix together the smoked paprika, cumin, garlic powder, coriander, cinnamon, oregano, mint and dill with the garlic and olive oil. Add the chicken pieces and mix well, then leave to marinate for at least 4 hours and ideally overnight.

Set your oven to at least 230°C. Put the onion halves on a foil-lined tray and push the skewers into them so they're pointing up. Push the marinated chicken pieces down onto the skewers so they are packed tight and flat. Put the tray on the bottom shelf in the oven with the skewers are still pointing up, and cook the chicken for about 30 minutes, until it is charred all over with an internal temperature of 75°C.

My Favourite Cheeseburger

A cheeseburger is possibly my all-time fave food, the kind of thing I'll request on my birthday or when I feel like indulging. The US has it locked on the burger front. When I was working at Gordon Ramsey's, all the boys would often go out for beers after our shift. We'd always end up eating somewhere, making it just before the 2am last call at Corner Bistro or the burger joint at the Parker Meridian to get food before they closed. Corner Bistro did the simplest but most brilliantly executed cheeseburger: nothing more complex than burger, American cheese, pickles and a squishy bun – and absolutely no salad. Who likes hot salad? It was the best.

Serves 4

4 Brioche Burger Buns (page 238)
30g tomato ketchup
15g sweet yellow mustard
30g mayonnaise
12 slices dill pickles

....

8 Burgers (recipe follows)
vegetable oil
salt

....

8 American cheese slices
1 recipe Caramelised Onions (recipe follows)

....

2 large cast-iron frying pans

Prepare your buns before you start cooking; it's much easier. Cut them across in half and spread a couple of circles' worth of ketchup, mustard and mayo on both halves of each bun. I don't mix them beforehand like a special sauce; I like to keep them separate so you get different bites each time. Place three pieces of dill pickle on the bottom buns.

Because each sandwich gets two burgers, ideally you want to heat up two cast-iron pans so you can cook all the burgers at the same time, four in each pan. Once the pans are as hot as can be, brush the burgers with a little vegetable oil. This will help them not to stick, but don't use a lot as you want the burgers to colour nicely. Salt them evenly, then fry for about 2 minutes.

Flip all the burgers over and put a slice of cheese on each one, and then a spoonful of caramelised onion on four of them. Fry for another 2 minutes until the cheese melts slightly, then stack two burgers on each bun-bottom, ensuring each stack gets one burger with onions and one without. Put on the bun tops and enjoy straightaway.

Recipes continue on page 39

CORNER
BISTRO
ONE WAY
ONE WAY

Burgers

Makes 8 × 85g burgers

Ask your local butcher to grind these cuts in a mincer for you, ideally through a medium-small mincer die.

400g shoulder steak, minced
230g short rib, minced
50g beef fat, minced

vegetable oil

Mix together the steak, short rib and minced beef fat and weigh it into eight 85g balls. On a piece of clingfilm brushed with a little vegetable oil, flatten each ball into a patty about 1 to 2cm thick. I like a thinner burger, double-stacked. Cover with baking parchment and wrap tightly with clingfilm, then keep in the fridge for up to 2 days.

Remove the burgers from the fridge at least 30 minutes before you cook them to get up to room temperature – this will make them cook more evenly.

Caramelised Onions

Serves 4

80g vegetable oil
3 large white onions, peeled, halved and thinly sliced

40g butter
10g sugar
6g salt

Heat a pan to a medium heat and add the vegetable oil and the onion. Start to sweat the onions down, then once they are a little translucent add the butter and season with the sugar and salt.

Continue to cook, reducing the heat if the onions begin to stick to the bottom of the pan. Once they are nice and caramel-coloured – about 20 minutes – take the pan off the heat and leave to cool.

Buttermilk Fried Chicken, Waffles, Honey Butter

Everyone loves fried chicken! This recipe is inspired by a meal I ate at WD-50 in NYC, where Wylie Dufresne did cold fried chicken with ricotta and caviar. The combo was so good. We had this on the menu at Noto for a bit and everyone loved it, but we had to take it off because we just couldn't make waffles fast enough on our tiny little machine. The honey butter is more of a traditional southern American thing and completes the dish for me.

Serves 4

1 recipe Buttermilk Fried Chicken (recipe follows)
4 Waffles (recipe follows)
1 recipe Honey Butter (recipe follows)
50g créme frâiche
20g Exmoor caviar
10g chives, finely chopped

Place a piece of fried chicken on a waffle triangle. Top with warm honey butter and garnish with créme frâiche, caviar and finely chopped chives.

Buttermilk Fried Chicken

Serves 2–4

Use chicken on the bone or off; it's up to you.

4 skinless chicken wings, thighs and/or drumsticks

85g buttermilk

100g plain flour
50g cornflakes, crushed
3g salt

vegetable oil to deep fry

If you are using boneless pieces of chicken, you need to flatten them first. Cover a board with clingfilm, then place a chicken piece flat on top and cover with another layer of clingfilm. With a mallet or saucepan, flatten the chicken to a thickness of 5mm. Put the chicken pieces in a bowl and pour over the buttermilk. Refrigerate for 24 hours.

Remove the chicken from the buttermilk and pat dry to remove any excess moisture. In a shallow bowl, mix the flour with the cornflakes and salt. Place a piece of chicken in the mix and press it down firmly, then flip it and repeat until the chicken is well coated. Repeat with the remaining pieces.

Heat a deep fryer or air fryer to 180°C and cook the chicken a few pieces at a time for 5 minutes, or until golden brown and a probe shows an internal temperature of 65°C. Drain on paper towels and season lightly with additional salt. Make sure you allow the oil to return to a temperature of 180°C before cooking the next batch.

Recipes continue on page 42

Waffles

Makes 8 waffles

150g self-raising flour
5g baking powder
5g salt

1 egg

240g milk

In a bowl, whisk together the flour, baking powder and salt. Add the egg and mix to form a paste, then slowly pour in the milk while mixing to form a smooth batter.

Cook the waffles in a well-greased preheated iron as per the manufacturer's instructions, until golden brown.

Honey Butter

Makes 250g

100g honey

200g cold butter, diced

sherry vinegar
salt

In a pot, heat the honey and reduce to a tacky consistency, about 5 or 6 minutes.

Turn the heat to low, then slowly whisk in the butter a couple of pieces at a time so the sauce emulsifies, adding a small amount of water as necessary if it becomes too thick. Season with sherry vinegar and salt as needed.

Tête de Cochon Terrine

Chef Markus Glocker taught me how to make this dish. At Gordon Ramsay we used to do it with veal heads with a rich sauce of wine and shallots, but I changed it to use pork – which is more readily available – seasoned with pastrami spice as a nod to American cuisine.

Serves 4

200g plain flour
4 eggs, whisked
500g fine panko breadcrumbs
4 pieces Tête de Cochon (recipe follows)

....

50g Mustard Emulsion (page232)
12 pieces Pickled Silverskin Onions (page 223)
10g Pickled Mustard Seeds (page 222)
20g crisp Granny Smith apple, cut into thin matchsticks
50g Burnt Apple Ketchup (page 226)

Place the flour, eggs and half the panko breadcrumbs in three separate bowls. First dust the tête de cochon pieces in flour, ensuring that you tap off any excess, then coat in egg before finally crusting in panko, pressing the breadcrumbs in so the meat is thoroughly coated. Add fresh breadcrumbs to the bowl when the mixture starts to look clumpy.

Heat a deep fat fryer or air fryer to 180°C and fry the breaded tête de cochon pieces until golden brown and hot in the centre, 3 to 4 minutes. Drain on paper towels.

Place a piece of tête de cochon on the plate, then pipe mustard emulsion on top. Garnish with petals of pickled onion, pickled mustard seeds and apple, and place a spoonful of burnt apple ketchup alongside.

Recipes continue on page 44

Tête de Cochon

Makes 12 pieces

2kg pork jowl
30g Pastrami Spice (recipe follows)
15g salt

1.5L Roast Chicken Stock (page 52)

80g vegetable oil
4 shallots, finely chopped
15g ginger, finely chopped
2g ground Szechuan peppercorns
2g ground cardamom

250g sake
75g treacle
75g kecap manis
35g mirin
5g soy

salt
sugar
sherry vinegar

20 × 20cm baking tin

Generously rub the pork jowl with pastrami spice and salt. In the restaurants we vac pac it and then cook it in a water bath for 12 hours at 82°C. Alternatively, place the jowl in a slow cooker or cassoulet pot. Cover with the roast chicken stock (top it up with water if it doesn't cover the meat) and braise on a low heat overnight.

Once cooked, remove the jowl from the stock and roughly chop into 3 to 4cm pieces, then set aside to cool. Reserve the stock.

In a pot, heat the vegetable oil and then sweat the shallots and ginger with the ground Szechuan pepper and cardamom until the shallots begin to soften. Add the sake, treacle, kecap manis, mirin and soy and the reserved chicken stock, then reduce on low heat until it reaches a tacky consistency, about 30 minutes.

Pour the glaze over the jowl and massage it into the meat, then season as necessary with salt, sugar and sherry vinegar.

Double line your baking tin with clingfilm, and then press the meat tightly into it. Cover with more clingfilm and place a weight atop, then once it is completely cool refrigerate (with the weight in place) overnight.

The next day, turn the terrine out onto a cutting board and remove all the clingfilm. Cut it into twelve 9 × 3cm pieces (the trim works wonderfully in a stir fry, pasta bake or sandwich). You can store these, wrapped in clingfilm, in the freezer for up to a month.

Pastrami Spice

Makes 90g

28g black peppercorns
14g coriander seeds
20g brown sugar
8g smoked paprika
5g garlic powder
5g onion powder
5g yellow mustard seeds
5g mustard powder

In a spice grinder, blitz all the ingredients together into a fine powder. Store in an airtight container.

Gnudi, Spring Vegetables and Lemon Butter Sauce

The first time I had gnudi was when a friend took me to April Bloomfield's Spotted Pig in the West Village. A Michelin star pub from an English chef, it was one of the coolest places I had ever been. The signatures she was famous for at the time included a burger with Roquefort and also these soft pillowy cheese dumplings.

Serves 4

1 recipe Gnudi (recipe follows)
100g cold water
90g cold, unsalted butter, diced

45g Parmesan, grated

juice of 2 lemons
1 recipe Spring Vegetables (recipe follows)

2g chives, finely chopped
2g parsley, finely chopped
2g dill, finely chopped
2g chervil, finely chopped
salt

First, pro-glaze the gnudi. Put them into a large frying pan with the cold water and start to warm on a medium heat. Once the water begins to simmer, add the cold diced butter, swirling the pan as it cooks.

A butter emulsion should begin to form as the water starts to evaporate (3 to 4 minutes). Add the grated Parmesan to the pan and continue to cook and swirl; the sauce should begin to look glossy and start to coat the gnudi (about 1 minute).

Once the sauce has thickened, add the lemon juice and mix well to incorporate, then gently fold in the spring vegetables and continue to cook until everything is hot. If the sauce becomes too thick or begins to separate, add a small amount of warm water.

Just before serving, fold in the chopped herbs and season with salt and lemon juice as needed.

Gnudi

Serves 4

455g ricotta

50g plain flour
50g Parmesan, grated
1 egg yolk
½ whole nutmeg
zest of ½ lemon
salt

330g fine semolina

30g vegetable oil

In a sieve lined with muslin, hang the ricotta over a bowl for 4 hours.

Mix the dry ricotta with the flour, Parmesan and egg yolk. Season with a pinch of salt, some freshly grated nutmeg and the lemon zest.

Place the semolina flour on a large flat baking tray. Put a small bowl of water nearby and wet your fingers, then grab about a teaspoonful of the ricotta mixture and form it into a rough small dumpling. Place it on the tray of semolina and roll it around until it is completely covered. Repeat with the remaining ricotta mix.

At this point, you can either store the gnudi on the tray of semolina, tightly wrapped, in the fridge for 24 hours, or you can poach them immediately.

In a large pot of gently boiling salted water, poach the gnudi in two batches for 2 to 3 minutes until they float, then transfer to an ice bath to cool. Once completely cool, remove from the ice bath and lightly coat in vegetable oil to prevent sticking. Store in the fridge for up to 24 hours.

Spring Vegetables

Serves 4

300g tenderstem broccoli

300g courgettes

300g podded broad beans

Remove any woody stems from the broccoli, then blanch in boiling salted water until tender (1 to 3 minutes) and cool in an ice bath.

On a mandolin, slice the courgettes lengthways into thin sheets, then cut each sheet in half down its length and remove the seeds so you are left with long ribbons.

Blanch the broad beans in boiling salted water for 1 minute, then cool in an ice bath. Once cool, remove their outer skin.

Roast Chicken and Sweetcorn Succotash

We used to make this sweetcorn succotash when I worked under Neil Ferguson at The London. I love it with chicken. It is genius and very simple but shows how the combination of a few great ingredients with a little bit of contrast go together. The first succotash came from the Native Americans, who would make big pots of boiled corn, often including different vegetables.

Serves 4

- 1 whole free-range chicken, about 1.8kg in weight
- 15g olive oil
- 20g salt
- 10g thyme
- ½ lemon
- ½ bulb of garlic

....

- 1 recipe Sweetcorn Succotash (recipe follows)

....

- 1 recipe Chicken Sauce (recipe follows)

Preheat the oven to 200°C.

Place the chicken on a tray lined with tin foil and parchment. Rub all over with olive oil and then season with the salt both on the outside of the bird and inside the cavity.

Pick the thyme leaves off the stem and scatter over the chicken. Stuff the lemon and garlic into the cavity.

Turn the oven down to 190°C and roast the chicken for 70 minutes, then take it out and leave to rest, uncovered, for 15 minutes.

Carve up the chicken however you like and serve beside the sweetcorn, with plenty of sauce.

Sweetcorn Succotash

Serves 4

350g sweetcorn kernels, fresh if possible but frozen will do
200g chicken stock

100g Sweetcorn Purée (recipe follows)
2 green chillies, deseeded and finely chopped
6 cippolini onions or 2 shallots, thinly sliced

50g unsalted butter, diced

1 small Baby Gem lettuce, chopped
5g basil, finely chopped
2g tarragon, finely chopped
2g parsley, finely chopped
salt
sherry vinegar

Put the sweetcorn kernels and the chicken stock in a medium-sized pot on a medium heat. Bring to the boil, stirring regularly, and allow the stock to reduce down to about 50ml.

Add the sweetcorn purée, chilli and onions. It should be a little thick at this point but take it off the heat and fold in the butter, which will melt and loosen the mix. It will feel like a loose risotto – if it still feels thick add 15g water.

Return to a low heat and stir in the lettuce and herbs. Season with a little salt and the sherry vinegar to taste – don't be shy with it, you're looking for a sweet and sour kinda flavour.

Sweetcorn Purée

300g fresh or tinned sweetcorn

If you're using fresh sweetcorn, juice it and place the juice in a pan. Bring it to a boil: the natural corn starch will thicken it to a pudding consistency. If you're using tinned corn, drain it and then blend with a little water to get a thick purée.

If you're making the purée in advance, place clingfilm directly on the surface to prevent a skin from forming and refrigerate for up to 3 days.

Recipes continue on page 52

Chicken Sauce

Serves 4

250g Roast Chicken Stock (recipe follows)

10g unsalted butter, cold and diced
5g sherry vinegar

5g parsley, chopped
5g chervil, chopped

Place the stock in a small pan and reduce until it starts to thicken. Once it is close to coating the back of a spoon, take off the heat and whisk in the cold butter, then season with the sherry vinegar. Fold in the parsley and chervil when you are close to plating.

Roast Chicken Stock

Makes 1.5kg

2kg raw chicken carcasses and wings

10g vegetable oil
500g shallots, sliced
400g mushrooms, sliced
1 garlic clove, unpeeled and crushed
8 black peppercorns, crushed

300g white wine

2kg chicken stock

1 bay leaf
1 sprig thyme
½ sprig rosemary

Preheat the oven to 200°C.

Chop the chicken carcasses into small pieces and roast on trays in the oven for 20 to 25 minutes, until dark brown.

Heat a large pot to medium heat and add the oil. When it's hot, add the sliced shallots, mushrooms, garlic and peppercorns and cook until the shallots and mushrooms are caramelised. Deglaze with the wine, then add the roasted bones to the pot. Cover with chicken stock, bring to the boil and skim.

Add the bay leaf, thyme and rosemary and simmer for 30 minutes. Pass the stock through a fine chinois and reduce to the consistency you want, then taste and correct seasoning.

Note: The colouration of the bones and onions is very important. If they're too light the stock will be pale and flavourless; if too dark, it will be bitter.

Ice Cream Sandwich

Ice cream sandwiches are a quintessential American thing; the ones you find in the UK just don't compare. When we lived in NYC we would have these after dinner or when we were watching a movie and I miss them dearly: every time we go back to the States we make up for it. This is as close as I can make them to the American ones: the cookie is blended up to make a softer outer layer, and the ice cream should stay nice and soft and chewy.

Makes 6 sandwiches

50g unsalted butter, melted
½ recipe Graham Cracker Crust (recipe follows)

1 recipe Malted Barley Semifreddo (recipe follows)

6 × 9cm ring moulds
blowtorch

Add enough of the melted butter to the cracker crust to form a wet packable dough (if it's too oily, add a small dusting of icing sugar).

Put the ring moulds on a parchment-covered baking tray, and then tightly press enough dough into them to get a layer about 2mm thick. Freeze, then once cold remove the moulds and repeat the process to create another six biscuits. Leave these ones in the moulds.

As soon as the semifreddo is ready, pipe it into the ring moulds with the biscuit base at the bottom. Top with a second biscuit and freeze for at least 8 hours or preferably overnight.

To unmould the sandwiches, very lightly blowtorch around the edge of the mould and push them out. Return to the freezer until needed.

Recipes continue on page 56

Graham Cracker Crust

Makes 700g

100g unsalted butter, softened
220g soft light brown sugar

300g whole wheat flour
50g cocoa powder
4g baking powder
2g salt

45g milk
110g honey

Preheat the oven to 170°C.

In a stand mixer with the paddle attachment, beat the butter and sugar until light and fluffy. Add in the flour, cocoa, baking powder and salt and mix until thoroughly combined, then mix in the milk and honey. It will be a dryish, clumpy dough. Spread evenly on two baking trays lined with silicone baking mats.

Bake for 15 minutes, then remove from the oven and fold the edges of the mixture into the middle, then spread it to an even layer again. Return to the oven for another 15 minutes, then fold the mixture again to break up any big lumps and allow to cool.

Crush to a crumb consistency in a Thermomix and store in the fridge until needed.

Malted Barley Semifreddo

Serves 6

170g double cream
1g vanilla seed powder

40g egg yolks
30g sugar

50g egg whites
30g sugar
1g salt

50g malted barley extract

piping bag

Whip the cream and vanilla seed powder to stiff peaks, then place in the fridge until needed.

Over a bain marie, whisk together the egg yolks and sugar until it reaches ribbon stage, then set aside.

Again over the bain marie, whisk the egg whites, sugar and salt until they are light and fluffy and the sugar has dissolved, then remove from the heat and whisk until cold in a stand mixer. They should be shiny and stiff.

Gently fold the whites into the yolks in two batches, then fold in the cold whipped cream. Finally, fold in malted barley so it's well combined. Put the semifreddo into a piping bag and use immediately.

SOFT ICE CREAM
COTTON CANDY
ITALIAN ICES
ICE COLD
BEER
CHARCOAL
BROIL
Fried
Chicken
HOT Italian
SAUSAGE

MILK
SHAKE
PINA
COLADA
CHILI
NACHOS
HOT
DOG
CHEEZ
BURGER
TACOS, TACOS "EL SAB ZON"
"TACOS
DE
BISTECK
CARNE ENCHILADA
POTATOE
BALLS
SHRIMP

Aizle

I have spent more time in Aizle than I have anywhere else in my life. When we first opened, the menu cost £35 – it's so funny to think now, but I would write two different menus every day, and then I would give the guests surprise courses from each menu, so for instance some people would get the beef dish and others got the pork. I covered all the dietary requirements as well; it was chaos: the cheapest menu with the most amount of work possible.

These are some of the dishes we have served over the years – some are current, and some are from day one. I wanted to show what we do at Aizle, and to give an insight into the level of craft that goes into the cooking. If you're a young chef you might want to see my restaurant recipes exactly as we make them, so here they are. And if you're reading at home then you can pick and choose elements of a dish without making the whole thing.

Barbados to Edinburgh
2013–2016

By 2013 I was working as chef de cuisine at Sandy Lane in Barbados. It is an unspoilt island, hardly developed, and untouched in so many ways. A lot of the houses are low-sitting, so as not to obstruct the beautiful views of the coast. There are always sheep and goats tied up in gardens and nothing is polished or new-feeling; it has an authenticity to it, it's paradise but also people live and work there, which I always found enchanting.

Sandy Lane was a different planet: it's one of the most luxurious hotels in the world and also one of the most professional. They gave us a beautiful house right near the beach with its own garden, a marble staircase, and an extra bedroom for people to come and stay. It was like living a millionaire's lifestyle, particularly because Krystal and I don't come from money.

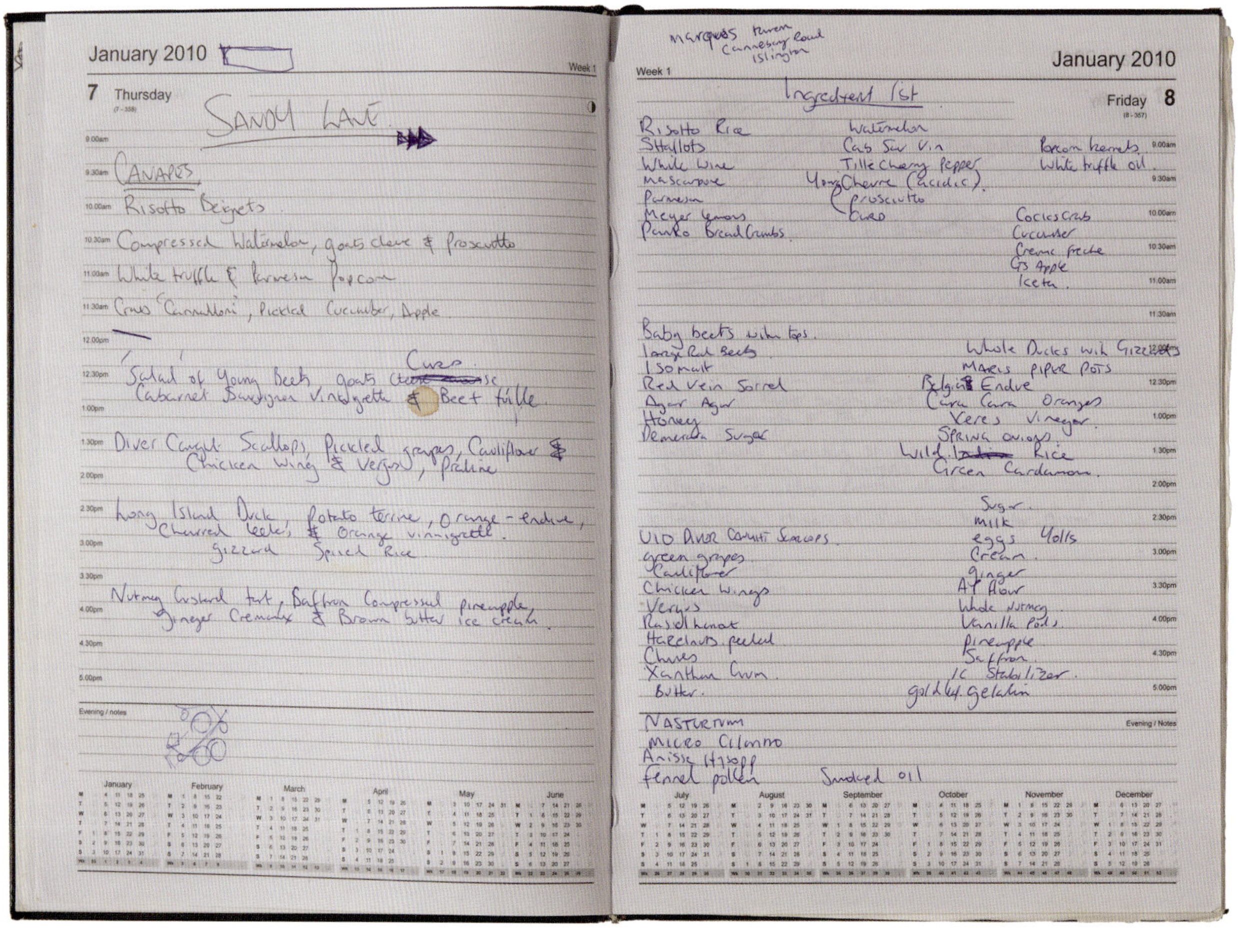

Moving to a predominantly black country really opened my eyes to a lot of things. I think all my local colleagues got on well with me because there was a mutual respect. The hotel had a history of employing expat chefs so the staff were used to the relationship and the dynamic but I don't think they liked it. They knew the expats were getting paid much more, and very few were bringing anything new to the table. Almost all the managers were foreign and mainly white, which in turn dredged up feelings from deep-rooted history.

The Executive Chef had run some of the world's biggest hotels and restaurants and was one of the hardest and most demanding chefs I'd worked under; he only wanted the best for the hotel and nothing could fall short of that. He was tough, but I really respected his drive and professionalism : he had very little time for excuses or anything that meant we weren't producing great food. He was also a fantastic cook; when he got on the stoves you could tell he wasn't full of shit.

I kept my mouth shut and just worked hard. I took my job seriously. There were always celebrities staying, like Rihanna and Mark Wahlberg, and in the summer every premiership footballer you could name. We spent our days off on the beach, we went on catamarans, drank rum punches and watched the sun go down. We had barbecues in the garden and listened to the frogs at night-time ribbit. Barbados was a bit of a dream, but eventually island life grew a little tiresome for both of us. We were still young, and living in Barbados isn't the same as holidaying in Barbados. We started talking about what to do next.

I remember Krystal and me bobbing up and down in the ocean and talking hypothetically about our plans for the future. She asked me what I wanted to do next – what would make me happy? I told her that this was the last time I could work for anybody. I wanted to open something casual where it was just me and a couple of other chefs cooking, somewhere cool and laid back, like the places we used to eat at in Brooklyn and downtown New York. A tasting-menu-only kind of place, a little rebellious, perhaps even with no menu and just a list of ingredients. And a set price that was accessible. No white tablecloths and posh service, something a bit more grungy.

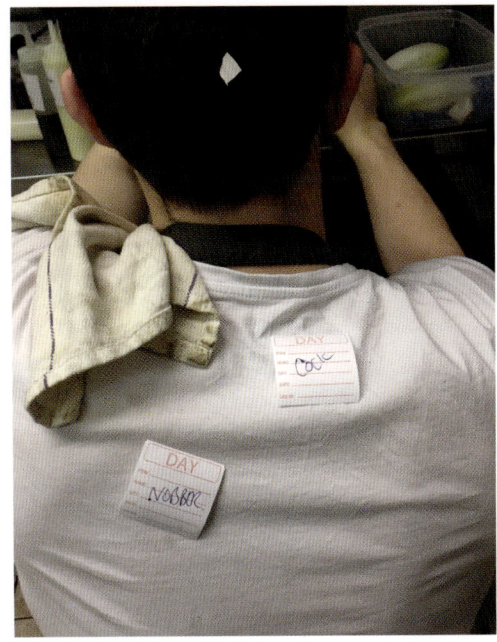

Right: Playing tricks on a young chef at the first Aizle.

Opposite: Using pages in a repurposed old diary to plan my Sandy Lane menu.

That was it. I bought a book called *How to Open Your First Restaurant* and set about writing my business plan. I was earning good money at Sandy Lane, so I could easily save and work towards the goal. We became obsessive about it – we got rid of our car, saved everything and started to plan our ideal restaurant.

I started emailing estate agents in Edinburgh and looking for sites, but all they had were million-pound properties. I searched constantly, and one day on a random Gumtree advert I found a restaurant for sale for £14,000 which was currently trading as a Chinese restaurant and takeaway. I looked at it on Google Maps – it seemed cute and overlooked Arthur's Seat, the huge volcanic rock just east of the city centre. My friend Brian scouted it for me and said it was a good idea so I booked a holiday from Sandy Lane and flew back to Edinburgh to look at the restaurant. When I got back to Barbados, I told Krystal I thought I could make it work, and after talking it over we decided to go for it. And so Aizle was born.

We moved back with £25,000 in savings. A family friend had worked at HSBC and helped set me up with a manager at the bank. They agreed to lend me £25,000 which meant I now had £50,000. I quickly realised that £50,000 was not a lot of money to open a restaurant with any sort of ambition. We naively thought that we could do the redecorating ourselves – this was surprising since neither of us could even

put up a shelf. We had joiners, restaurant fitters, designers and architects all give us quotes for the work, but as they mounted up into the hundreds of thousands, we decided just to hire a few key workmen who could get the place clean and tidy. With the help of them and a few friends we managed to get the restaurant looking half decent.

Still, we ran out of money pretty quickly. The last thing I managed to purchase was a 20-year-old stove that cost us £500. We had a few staff, a PR company to launch the restaurant and we were lucky that there were people willing to take a chance on us. Our wine supplier, Tarquin, agreed to stock the restaurant with wine and glasses and allowed me to pay for them over time to help our cashflow. This type of generosity was invaluable, and I'm happy to say he still supplies us today.

So the place was ready to open. It was decorated very simply with new paint, second-hand chairs, a few decent plates and some cheap cutlery. We had household fridges full of wine in the backroom, one fridge for the kitchen and two non-stick pans. That was it. I hired two chefs – Mark and Big Stu – and Krystal was going to run the front of house. We were young and passionate, and we blindly convinced ourselves it was going to work. My original idea for Aizle was to have no menu, just a list of the seasonal ingredients that we used on the tasting menu and I would change the dishes every day. In theory, this was a romantic and charming idea. In reality, it was a fucking nightmare. I was working like crazy and not thinking straight because there were so many things I had to manage. I hadn't practised any of the dishes and I didn't make anything I had cooked in previous restaurants. In a very out-of-control kind of way, I thought I was some sort of naturally gifted genius who could just come up with things off the top of my head. The cracks began to show very quickly.

We were all working too many hours and not making much money. I felt an enormous amount of pressure to be everything and to do everything myself, but I wasn't in control of anything. We tried to do as many covers in the restaurant as we could to give ourselves the best possible chance of survival. The success rates of restaurants don't make for great reading and the fear of failing terrified me so I just worked through everything.

Still, it was the best work experience of my life. When we first started, the menu was £35 for five courses, and when I look back at those early menus some still excite me, even today. I felt like there were no rules. I didn't care if someone said, 'You can't serve raw duck tartar; nobody will eat it.' I remember an old boss telling me not to open a restaurant with no menu and only 36 seats. To a large degree that's what's made me go through with it: I suppose I've always had a complex about not being good enough, but I've also always thought about things differently, and after some hard work I think that's worked out for me.

My point is, if you're prepared to work hard, take the risks and put everything into it, you'll make it work – and for me, that's what Aizle has always stood for.

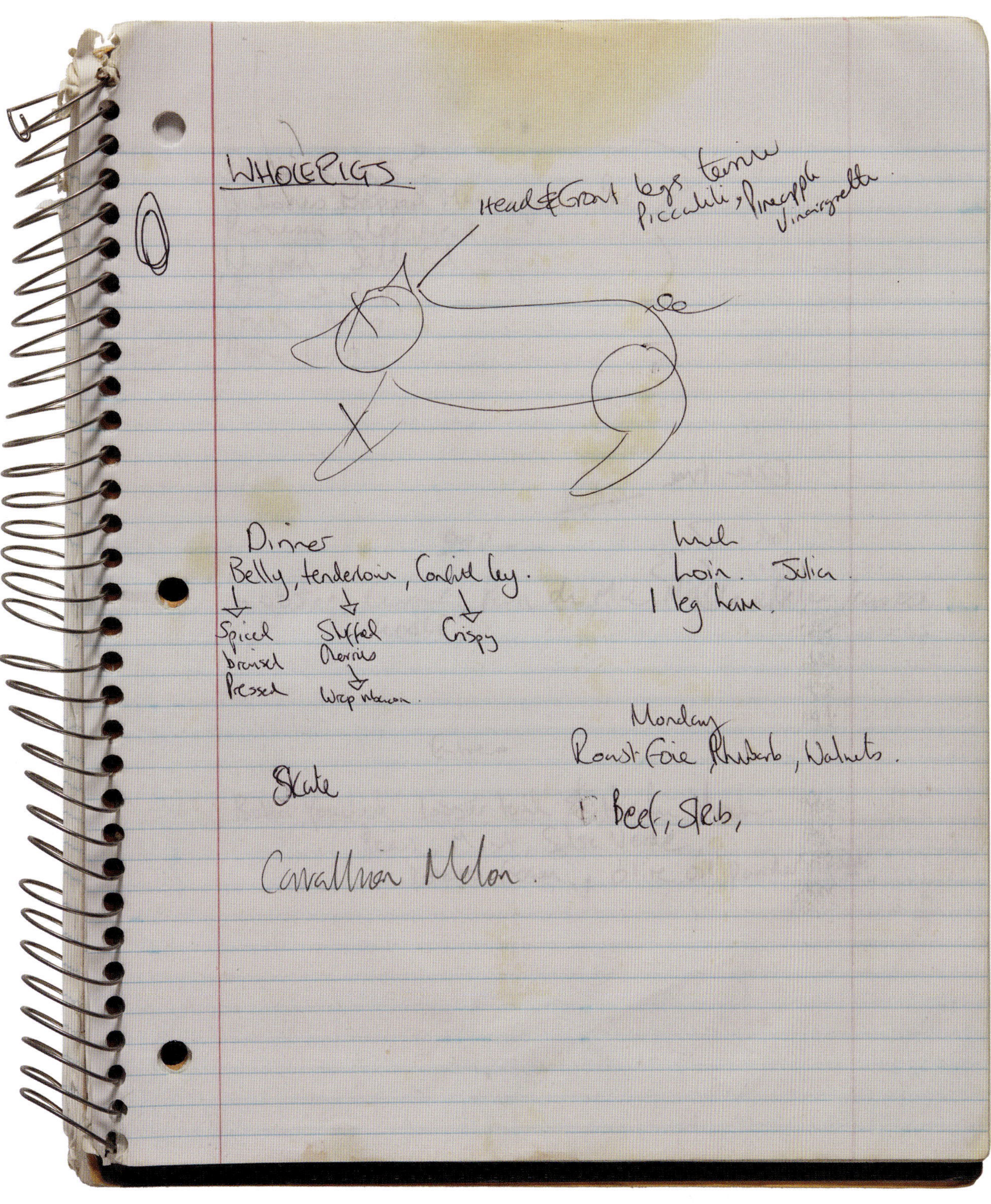

Above: A quick sketch of a pig to show how to use all the parts.

Opposite: Looking through the front door of the original Aizle.

Kombucha

Every night at Aizle we serve our customers a tumbler of our own kombucha, changing the flavourings seasonally with everything from sea buckthorn or ginger to pine or apple. It's an amazing fermented product, and I love how the green tea makes for a smooth vehicle to carry whatever different flavour we pair with it. Kombucha is very easy to manage and keep producing without having to waste money on supermarket versions, and you can get as creative as you like with flavours.

Makes 3 litres

500g water
16g loose leaf green tea (we use Genmaicha)

120g demerara sugar

1kg cold water

kombucha scoby
200g concentrated kombucha from a previous batch if you have some

2 × 3 litre jars

Our favourite flavourings:
250g grated ginger and 1 lemon, sliced
a handful of flowering currant and some fresh strawberries, sliced up
200g sea buckthorn berries and a spoonful of heather honey

Step 1

Heat the water to 80°C, then brew the green tea in it for 4 minutes.

Strain the tea into a large bowl and add the demerara sugar, stirring so it dissolves completely.

Top up with the cold water. Check the temperature of the mix – it should be no more than 24°C (warm to the touch, not hot).

Put the scoby and the concentrated kombucha (if you have some left from a previous batch) in a 3 litre jar and add the sweetened tea very gently so as not to disturb the scoby.

Top up with more cold water until the scoby or liquid is at the widest part of the top of the jar.

Cover the mouth of the jar with a double layer of j-cloth and leave to primary ferment for a week.

Step 2 (a week later)

Pour off three quarters of the fermented kombucha into a second 3 litre jar, leaving roughly 200ml kombucha behind with the scoby. To get your next batch going, add sweetened tea to the original jar and top up with cold water as per Step 1.

Add flavourings of your choice to the freshly fermented kombucha in the second jar, seal and leave to infuse at room temperature for 24 hours. Then you just need to strain it off and enjoy! We keep the finished product in the fridge so it doesn't continue to ferment.

Celeriac Tartlet, Sea Trout, Sour Cream, Sea Buckthorn

When I created this for the Great British Menu, Richard Corrigan gave it the top score of the canapés that day. The tartlet shell recipe was inspired by a dish in Bjorn Frantzen's cookbook. The filling is all our own though, with nods to Japanese flavours and Scottish produce.

Makes about 50 tarts

½ recipe Ponzu Gel (recipe follows)
1 recipe Celeriac Tart Shell (recipe follows)
1 recipe Sea Trout Tartar (recipe follows)
1 recipe Sour Cream Dome (recipe follows)

1 jar trout roe
100ml dry sake
20ml mirin

dill
cornflowers
fennel flowers

Pipe a little ponzu gel in the bottom of each tart shell, then fill it up with sea trout tartar. Top with a sour cream dome.

In a bowl, mix the trout roe with the dry sake and mirin and leave to marinate for 2 to 3 minutes.

Arrange the dill and flowers around the side of the tart and top with the marinated roe.

Ponzu Gel

Makes about 400g

This makes more than you need, but it's difficult to blend smooth if you make any less.

180g white soy
100g sea buckthorn juice
80g apple juice
50g mirin
80g sugar

5g katsuobushi

8g agar agar

In a large pan, combine the white soy, sea buckthorn juice, apple juice, mirin and sugar. Bring to the boil and then add the katsuobushi and leave to infuse for 20 minutes off the heat.

Strain and measure 400g into a medium pot. Add the agar and bring to a boil, constantly whisking for 2 to 3 minutes. Pour into a tray to set.

Once cool, it should be quite a firm jelly. Chop it up and blend until it is a smooth gel. Keep in the fridge for up to 7 days.

Celeriac Tart Shell

Makes about 50

325g celeriac

18g cornflour
26g isomalt
14g glucose powder
3g dulse powder

vegetable oil

40mm tart moulds

Peel and dice the celeriac into small cubes. Put in a pot, cover with water and boil until soft, then drain in a colander and blend up into a smooth purée.

Mix the celeriac with the cornflour, isomalt, glucose powder and dulse in a small pot and cook out into a paste (about 3 to 4 minutes). Spread the mixture thinly on a non-stick baking mat and dehydrate at 70°c for 1 to 2 hours, until tacky.

Preheat the oven to 90°C. Cut the celeriac into 5cm squares. Heat some vegetable oil to 80 to 90°C, then dip in the celeriac squares to make them pliable. Shape into tart shells in 40mm moulds and bake for 1 hour, then dehydrate at 55°C for another 12 hours.

Sea Trout Tartar

Makes 180g

150g Cured Trout (page 138)

5g red yuzu kosho
20g apple, peeled and cut into small dice
5g spring onion, cut into small dice
salt and lime juice to taste

We make our own yuzu kosho at Aizle. It's a fermented chilli paste that uses a mixture of citrus peel and chillies, blended into a paste and fermented. It adds a real savoury, deep flavour and a subtle heat that isn't burning. You don't have to make your own – you can buy some great ones online.

Cut the sea trout into very fine dice, then mix it with the red yuzu kosho, diced apple and diced spring onion. Season with salt and lime juice to taste.

Sour Cream Dome

Makes 250g

250g sour cream
1.5g agar agar
0.5g xanthan gum
lemon juice
salt

20mm hemispherical silicone moulds

Combine the sour cream, agar agar and xanthan gum in a small pan and season with lemon juice and salt. Gently heat until the agar powder has melted and then bring to a gentle boil. Pour into 20mm hemispherical silicone moulds and leave somewhere cool to set. Pop the domes out when ready to use.

Onion Croustade

Possibly in my top five favourite snacks of all time, this small bite really packs a punch at the start of the meal. It's not a revolutionary pairing but is a bit of a modern take on a classic (Cheese and Onion is also my favourite flavour of crisps). Anster cheese is a slightly tangy, crumbly cheese that's very versatile and is made in Fife, like all great things (it's where I grew up #FIFE4LIFE).

The croustades are simple to make if you have an iron, which you can easily find online.

Makes about 20

1 recipe Croustade (recipe follows)
100g Onion Fondue (recipe follows)
½ recipe Anster Cheese Espuma (recipe follows)
100 Pickled Wild Leek Buds (page 225)
wild garlic powder

Fill the croustades with onion fondue. Top with Anster cheese espuma, some pickled wild leek buds and a little wild garlic powder.

Croustade

Makes about 20

100g gluten-free plain flour
100g Pilsner
80g water
1 egg
15g melted unsalted butter
7g sugar
7g salt

10g squid ink

vegetable oil to deep fry

Combine the flour with the Pilsner, water, egg, melted butter, sugar and salt. Whisk into a smooth batter, then add enough squid ink to make it jet black. Refrigerate the batter and allow it to rest for a minimum of 2 hours and ideally overnight.

Heat the vegetable oil to 170°C. Heat a croustade iron in the oil, then dip it into the batter and put back into the oil. The batter will stick to the hot iron, then release into the hot oil once it is cooked. Remove with a slotted spoon onto kitchen towel and heat the iron again before making the next croustade. These will stay fresh for a day.

Recipes continue on page 72

Onion Fondue

Makes about 450g

80g vegetable oil
3 large white onions, thinly sliced
1 sprig of thyme

15g unsalted butter
5–10g sherry vinegar to taste
salt

In a large pan, add enough vegetable oil to just cover the bottom. On a low heat, sweat the onions with the thyme until they have hardly any colour but are very soft in texture, about 90 minutes.

Once cooked, add the butter and season with sherry vinegar and salt.

Anster Cheese Espuma

Makes enough to fill an iSi siphon gun

450g double cream

170g Anster cheese, grated
125g mascarpone

Place the cream in a pot and reduce by a third over a medium heat. Add in the Anster cheese and mascarpone, then put in a Thermomix at 70°C for 5 minutes to melt.

Put the cheese mixture in an iSi siphon gun and charge with one N_2O charger. Keep warm in a water bath set to 50°C, shaking regularly.

Truffle Chawanmushi, Mushrooms, Berkswell Cheese

We must have made millions of chawanmushis by now as we've served this at Aizle since day one. Over the years we've gone through tons of flavour combinations, but this one really stands out. It's a fairly classic combination as far as cheese, mushrooms and truffles go, and we present the dish in beautiful autumnal baskets made for us by Fiona from Pyrus Botanicals in Edinburgh. She grows or forages, cuts and dries all of the foliage and then weaves it into baskets. We update them two or three times a year so they change with the seasons.

Serves 6

1 recipe Truffle Chawanmushi (recipe follows)
120g Cep Purée (recipe follows)
1 recipe Roasted Mushrooms (recipe follows)
½ recipe Sherry Vinegar Jelly (recipe follows)
1 recipe Croutons (recipe follows)
1 recipe Berkswell Espuma (recipe follows)
1 recipe Mushroom Leaf Crisps (recipe follows)
50g micro nasturtiums
10g cep powder
....
10g truffles, finely sliced

Take the warm, steamed chawanmushi and top each one with dots of cep purée. Scatter roasted mushrooms around the dish, then add some sherry vinegar gel dice and a few croutons. Place some of the Berkswell espuma – about the size of a golf ball – to the side and scatter the leaf crisps and nasturtiums over the top. Dust everything with a little cep powder.

If you're feeling that little bit extra baller, finish with sliced fresh truffles.

Recipes continue on page 76

Truffle Chawanmushi

Makes 6

185g milk
185g cream
2.5g truffle peelings from a jar
15g soy
10g salt
4 large eggs

six small bowls or ramekins

Mix the milk, cream, truffle peelings, soy, salt and eggs in a bowl and whisk until smooth. Check the seasoning and adjust to taste.

Pour 80g of the mix into each bowl and tightly wrap the top in clingfilm. Steam the chawanmushi in a bamboo steamer for about 8 to 10 minutes until set, or cook in a bain marie in the oven at 90°C: it should wobble slightly but not look like it would pour.

Cep Purée

Makes 350g

This makes more than you need, but you can't blend to a smooth purée with any less.

100ml vegetable oil
250g frozen ceps, defrosted and drained
200g button mushrooms, sliced

a splash of sherry vinegar
250g chicken stock

150ml double cream

2g xanthan gum

salt

Heat the vegetable oil in a medium-sized pot. Once hot, add both the ceps and button mushrooms and roast on a high heat until they are all a golden caramel colour.

Deglaze the bottom of the pot with a splash of sherry vinegar and add the chicken stock.

Lower the heat a bit and cook out until the mushrooms are soft (about 30 minutes) then add the cream and cook for a further 10 minutes.

Transfer to a blender and blend with the xanthan gum (which will thicken the purée). When it's nice and smooth, check the seasoning, then pass it through a fine sieve to remove any lumps. You should be left with a silky smooth purée.

Roasted Mushrooms

Serves 6

50g vegetable oil
200g maitake mushrooms
200g chanterelles or girolles
100g large king oyster mushrooms

100g unsalted butter, diced
2 peeled, whole garlic cloves
2 sprigs thyme

salt

You can use any mixture of mushrooms you can get your hands on. That's the beauty of the dish: its flavour profile constantly changes according to the mushrooms in season.

Heat the oil in a deep, medium-sized saucepan, then add the mushrooms and roast for 5 to 8 minutes, moving them continuously so they get an even golden colour. Once golden, add the butter, garlic and thyme and continue to cook for 3 to 4 minutes whilst moving everything around the pan. This will improve the colour and the flavour. Season with a little salt.

Sherry Vinegar Jelly

Makes about 250g

95g water
95g sherry vinegar
75g caster sugar
3g agar agar

Place the water, sherry vinegar, sugar and agar in a small pot and bring to a boil, continuously whisking. After 2 minutes, pour into a small container to set at room temperature – it should set up within 30 minutes. Turn out the jelly and cut into small 5mm dice ready to serve.

Croutons

Makes about 150g

3 slices of brioche

50ml vegetable oil
100g unsalted butter, diced

2 garlic cloves, peeled and squashed
2 sprigs thyme

salt

Cut the brioche into 1cm cubes.

Heat the oil in a deep medium-sized saucepan, then add the butter and get it hot and foaming. Add in the brioche cubes and roast in the foaming butter for 5 to 8 minutes, moving continuously so they get an even golden colour.

Once golden, add the garlic and thyme and infuse for a further 2 minutes off the heat, then drain the excess butter off through a sieve and lay the croutons on a paper towel to dry.

Season whilst hot with a little salt.

Berkswell Espuma

Fills 1 iSi siphon gun

450g double cream

125g mascarpone
170g Berkswell cheese, grated

Place the cream into a medium-sized pot and begin to gently simmer over a medium heat until it has reduced by half.

Add in the mascarpone and grated Berkswell cheese, then place into a blender and blend until smooth.

Transfer to an iSi siphon gun and charge with one shot of N_2O, then keep it warm in a water bath set to 50°C.

Mushroom Leaf Crisps

Makes about 535g

This makes more than you need.

500g sweet potatoes

125g T55 flour
75g egg white
25g trisol
10g salt

leaf-shaped moulds

Preheat the oven to 160°C.

Place the sweet potatoes on a baking tray and cook in the oven for about 1 hour, or until they are soft. Scoop out the insides and reserve 300g. Turn the oven down to 150°C.

Put the reserved baked sweet potato into a blender with the T55 flour, egg white, trisol and salt. Blend until you have a smooth paste. You can freeze any excess at this point.

Spread the paste onto leaf-shaped moulds and bake for 10 minutes.

Pop the leaves out of the moulds whilst still warm and keep aside.

Sheep's Milk Agnolotti, Parmesan Consommé

One of the best things I learned at Gordon Ramsay was how to make great pasta. We would have to have three doughs resting by 8am, ready for the head chef to start making lobster ravioli, rabbit tortellini and linguine at 9am, fresh every day.

Serves 6

1 recipe Parmesan Consommé (recipe follows)

18 pieces Sheep's Milk Agnolotti (recipe follows)

1 recipe Wild Garlic Pesto (recipe follows)

Pickled Wild Leeks (page 223)

2g alyssum
2g mustard frill
2g toasted pine nuts

Bring the Parmesan consommé to a simmer and re-season as necessary.

Blanch the agnolotti in a large pot of boiling salted water until cooked, approximately 2 minutes. Remove with a slotted spoon and place three agnolotti in each bowl, then put a little pesto on each one.

Take your pickled wild leeks out of the liquor, chop into 5cm lengths, and arrange on the pasta. Garnish with alyssum, mustard frill and a few toasted pine nuts and serve, pouring over the Parmesan consommé at the table.

Parmesan Consommé

Makes about 500g

You can freeze any you don't use.

100g vegetable oil
1 banana shallot, sliced
½ leek (white only), sliced
2 cloves garlic, chopped
1 sprig thyme
1 Parmesan rind

50g white wine
1.5kg water
200g parmesan, grated

4 egg whites, at room temperature

In a large pot, heat the vegetable oil, then sweat off the shallot, leek, garlic, thyme and Parmesan rind until soft but not coloured, roughly 6 to 7 minutes. Deglaze with the white wine, then add the water and grated Parmesan.

Bring to a boil, then reduce the heat to low and cook out for 3 hours. Pass through a muslin cloth into a bowl.

To clarify, warm the stock to 80°C. Lightly whisk the egg whites, then whisk them into the stock and continue to heat gently until they form a raft. Make a hole in the centre and continue to cook on a low heat for approximately 90 minutes.

Check the stock is clear by ladling some out through the hole in the centre of the raft. When it's ready, ladle out all of the stock and pass it through a muslin cloth, leaving the raft in the pot. The stock should now be very clear. Season to taste.

Recipes contine on page 80

Sheep's Milk Agnolotti

Makes 70–80

In the restaurant, we serve three agnolotti per portion but at home the full recipe will serve 2 to 4.

1 recipe Pasta Dough (recipe follows)
a little 00 flour
a little fine semolina

1 recipe Ricotta Filling (recipe follows)

1 egg, lightly beaten

Cut the rested pasta dough in half and press each piece into a flat disc. Begin feeding the dough through the largest setting on the pasta machine, adding a small amount of 00 pasta flour if necessary to prevent sticking. Fold the dough in half lengthways and feed through the machine again, then repeat, reducing the setting each time until you reach the second finest (1.5 on our machine).

You should now have a long sheet of pasta. Lay it on a large work surface dusted with fine semolina.

Put the ricotta filling into a piping bag with an 8mm straight piping tip, pressing to remove any air bubbles. In one smooth motion, pipe the ricotta in a line along the centre of the pasta dough. Lightly brush the dough directly above the ricotta with egg wash.

Starting in the centre of the sheet of pasta, roll the bottom edge over the filling to meet the egg-washed top edge, and press gently to seal. Using a fluted pastry wheel, cut off the excess dough from the top, leaving a 2mm lip. Then, starting 5cm in front of the pasta, roll the pastry wheel straight through the filled pasta at 2cm increments to form individual agnolotti.

Check that each agnolotti is properly sealed and there are no holes or tears in the dough, then place on a tray generously dusted in fine semolina. Repeat with the second half of dough. Allow to rest uncovered for 2 hours.

Pasta Dough

Makes about 200g

large pinch of saffron threads
50g hot water

150g 00 flour
3 egg yolks

Steep the saffron threads in the hot water and allow to cool completely.

Put the flour in a food processor, turn the speed to high and add the egg yolks one by one. Slowly add enough saffron water for a dough to form, about 20 to 30g.

Knead the dough on an un-floured surface until smooth, then wrap in clingfilm and allow to rest for at least 1 hour in the fridge.

Ricotta Filling

Makes 400g

350g ricotta

50g Parmesan, grated
zest and juice of ½ lemon
grated nutmeg
salt and pepper

In a sieve lined with muslin, hang the ricotta over a bowl overnight.

The next day, combine the hung ricotta, Parmesan, lemon zest and juice in a bowl and season to taste with the nutmeg, salt and pepper.

Wild Garlic Pesto

Makes about 250g

100g wild garlic
25g pine nuts, toasted
zest and juice of 1 lemon
25g Parmesan, grated
100g pomace oil
salt and pepper

In a blender or food processor, blend half of the wild garlic with the toasted pine nuts, lemon zest and juice, Parmesan and about 35g of the oil.

Add the remaining wild garlic, then pulse whilst adding the rest of the oil until a coarse pesto is formed. Season to taste. Store in an airtight container in the fridge, covered in a layer of oil.

Wild Halibut, Summer Vegetables, Elderflower

This is from the early days of Aizle. We used to put it on as a starter in early summer when the elderflower comes out, and it shows just how well seasonal produce goes together. The cooking method is a great way to prepare any meaty fish at home.

Serves 4

80g olive oil
1 recipe Cured Halibut (recipe follows)

250g Roast Chicken Stock (page 52)
30g cold unsalted butter, diced

2g dill, chopped
2g tarragon, chopped
2g parsley, chopped
2–3 drops lemon juice

1 recipe Broad Bean Ragout (recipe follows)

1 recipe Elderflower Sabayon (recipe follows)
10g fresh herbs (we use chervil, dill and sea purslane)

Heat a non-stick pan with a little olive oil over a medium heat. Place the cured halibut pieces in the pan and sear on one side for 3 minutes on a medium heat, until golden and slightly crusted on the bottom.

Turn the fish over and add the chicken stock and butter. Cook and baste for another 3 minutes, then add the dill, tarragon and parsley, shaking the pan. Glaze the fish with the butter and stock emulsion in the pan, and finish with lemon juice.

Spoon some of the broad bean ragout in the middle of each plate.

Place the fish on top and finish with the whipped elderflower sabayon and some fresh herbs.

Cured Halibut

Makes 4 × 80g portions

150g sugar
150g salt

1 fillet wild halibut (approx. 350g), skinned

Mix the sugar and salt together. Place the halibut on a tray and cover all over with the sugar/salt mix, then put it in the fridge for 20 minutes.

Wash off the salt and sugar, then dry the fish on kitchen towel and portion it into four equal pieces weighing about 80 to 90g each.

Recipes continue on page 84

Broad Bean Ragout

Serves 4

1 green courgette

125g broad beans

2 shallots, sliced
50g vegetable oil
500g surf clams
50g white wine

180g Watercress Sauce (recipe follows)
salt

Cut the courgette in four lengthways, discard the seeds and dice the flesh into 5mm cubes.

Blanch the broad beans in boiling salted water for 2 to 3 minutes and cool in an ice bath. When they're cool, pop the broad beans from their outer skin.

In a pot, sweat the shallots in the vegetable oil until tender. Add the clams and the white wine, then cover and cook for 1 to 2 minutes, shaking the pot, until the clams all open. Strain and reserve the clam juice. Once cool, remove the clams from their shells.

Just before serving, mix the diced courgette, broad beans, watercress sauce and four tablespoons of the surf clams together and bring up to a medium-high heat in a small sauce pot, then adjust the seasoning with salt and clam juice.

Watercress Sauce

Makes 200g

80g parsley, leaves picked and chopped
80g mint, leaves picked and chopped
135g watercress, chopped

2 garlic cloves, chopped
150g olive oil
salt

Blanch the parsley, mint and watercress in boiling water for 30 seconds, then immediately drain and place into some iced water.

Squeeze the herbs dry and blend with garlic and olive oil to make a green herb purée. Add salt to taste.

Elderflower Sabayon

Fills 1 iSi siphon gun

36g egg yolk
25g elderflower vinegar

50g water
180g olive oil
salt

Place the egg yolks, vinegar, and a pinch of salt in a medium heatproof bowl set over a pan of simmering water.

Whisk constantly until the mixture has thickened, 2 to 3 minutes. As it's cooking, remove the bowl from the pan from time to time to prevent the sabayon from getting too hot and curdling.

When the eggs form a ribbon with a whisk, remove from the heat and adjust the consistency with up to 50g water so the sauce coats the back of a spoon. Slowly whisk in the olive oil until emulsified. Season with a little salt.

You can use it as a sauce as is, but I like to charge it in an iSi siphon gun – I love the height and lightness it gets from the espuma. Keep it at room temperature in a warm place until serving.

Lobster, Kohlrabi, Yoghurt

This has never actually been on the menu. It started off as the fish dish for the Great British Menu, then back in Scotland I thought about it and cooked it differently. I prefer this version.

Lobster really lends itself to barbecuing as it's robust and meaty. You need a few licks of hot charcoal to get a little caramelisation, but be quite gentle so you don't overcook it. Even if you don't make any other part of this recipe, that's the main thing to take away – barbecue your lobster!

Serves 2

2 Lobster Tails (recipe follows)

½ recipe Lobster Sauce (recipe follows)
6 Lobster Knuckle-stuffed Onions (recipe follows)
½ recipe Fermented Tomato Gel (recipe follows)
1 recipe Kohlrabi Purée (recipe follows)
2g micro shiso
5g sea purslane
5g fennel fronds

We barbecue the lobster tails on a Konro grill. Gently brush the tails with a little pomace oil and cook on a hot barbecue for 2 to 3 minutes each side.

Place a lobster tail next to a spoon of the lobster sauce on each plate. Heat up the stuffed onion petals under a grill until warm, then place three on the plate and top with a little fermented tomato gel. Place dots of kohlrabi purée around the onions, then decorate with a few leaves of micro shiso, sea purslane and fennel and serve with a cup of the lobster sauce on the side.

Lobster Tails

Serves 2

2 whole lobster

Put the lobster in the freezer until they're asleep, then push the tip of a knife through the cross on the back of the neck to kill them.

Take off the tail by twisting it and the lobster body in opposite directions. Remove the intestine pipe by twisting the middle fin on the bottle of the tail and gently pulling it. The pipe should come out in one piece. Twist off the claws, then chop up the body – shell and all – and set aside to make the sauce.

Blanch the lobster tails and claws in salted boiling water – the tails for 3 minutes and the claws for 5 minutes – then place in iced water to chill. Once cold, crack the tail open with your hands and remove the tail meat in one piece. Use the back of a knife to crack open the claws and get at the knuckle meat, which you will need for the stuffed onions recipe that follows.

Recipes continue on page 88

Lobster Sauce

Makes about 600-700g

This makes more than you need, but you can freeze the excess.

100g vegetable oil
300g chopped lobster shells

50g unsalted butter

200g white wine or mussel stock
375g chicken stock

80g olive oil
75g shallots, chopped
2 garlic cloves
75g carrots, chopped
75g celery, chopped
1 bay leaf
5g thyme

15g tomato purée

80g Noilly Prat

110g double cream
10g lemon juice

20g brandy
5g red yuzu kosho

First make a lobster stock. Heat a large pot and add the vegetable oil and lobster shells. Roast until the shells are bright pink and roasted, around 10 minutes. Add in the butter and whilst it foams move the bones around to get an even colouring. Deglaze with wine or mussel stock and reduce until the liquid is almost all absorbed. Top up the pot with the chicken stock and cook out for 40 minutes on a gentle simmer. Strain off and pass through a sieve, then set the lobster stock aside.

Heat a medium-sized pot and add the olive oil. Over a medium heat, sweat the shallots, garlic, carrots, celery, bay leaf and thyme until they're slightly translucent with no colour, about 10 minutes. Add the tomato purée and roast for a few minutes more, then add the Noilly Prat and reduce until absorbed. Add the lobster stock and cook out until the liquid is reduced by half and all the vegetables are cooked.

Transfer to a tall blender and blend until smooth, then add the double cream and lemon juice and pass the sauce through a chinois. Finally, stir in the brandy and yuzu kosho.

Lobster Knuckle-stuffed Onions

Makes about 9

80g pearl onions

60g reserved lobster knuckle meat (from Lobster Tails, page 86), chopped
20g Greek yoghurt
5g dill, finely chopped
5g chives, finely chopped
2g lemon zest
2g lemon juice
salt and black pepper

Gently steam the onions in their skins for 10 minutes until soft. Peel and separate them into individual petals.

Mix the lobster knuckle with the yogurt, dill, chives and lemon zest and juice and season to taste. Stuff each onion petal with about 10g of the lobster mix and place on a tray until ready to plate.

Fermented Tomato Gel

Makes about 300g

250g Fermented Tomato Water (recipe follows)
5g agar agar

38g soy sauce
13g sugar
8g white wine vinegar
10g katsuobushi
6g mirin

In a pot, mix the fermented tomato water and agar agar together until the agar has dissolved. Bring to a boil while constantly whisking and then cook out for 3 minutes. Add the soy sauce, sugar, white wine vinegar, katsuobushi and mirin and leave to infuse for 10 minutes.

Strain through a sieve and leave to go cold and set as a hard gel, then blend into a smooth gel consistency.

Fermented Tomato Water

Makes about 500g

800g plum tomatoes
30g basil
50g chervil
50g flat leaf parsley
2 sprigs thyme
1 shallot, chopped
1 garlic clove, chopped
80g white wine
15g salt

Chop the tomatoes into 2cm dice and put in a large bowl. Add the herbs, shallot, garlic, white wine and salt and leave to marinate for an hour, then pulse in a blender until pulpy but not smooth.

Line a colander with cheesecloth and pour in the tomato mixture. Let it drip slowly through the cloth into a bowl for at least 2 hours. The end result is a clarified clear liquid – to keep it clear, don't press the solids down in the cheesecloth, just leave them to drip.

Vacuum pack the liquid and leave in a warm place for 4 to 5 days. You will see it develop some fizziness and bubbles as it ferments.

Kohlrabi Purée

Makes about 450g

This makes more than you need, but you can freeze the excess.

500g kohlrabi, peeled and chopped small

6g agar agar
8g chardonnay vinegar
salt and white pepper to taste

5g grapeseed oil

Place the kohlrabi in a pot and cover with water, then cook on a high heat until it is very soft and has a mash-like texture. Drain off any excess water and transfer the kohlrabi to a Thermomix. Blend until smooth.

Add the purée into a pan with the agar agar and chardonnay vinegar and season with salt and white pepper to taste. Bring everything to a boil for 3 minutes, constantly whisking, then pour into a tray to cool and set into a hard gel. Once set, return it to the Thermomix with the oil and blend to make a smooth purée.

Wild Turbot, Razor Clams, Pickled Cucumber, Sauce Vin Blanc, Exmoor Caviar

This dish is a classic Aizle fish course. I generally serve most fish with a reduced fish-stock-based sauce, finished with a little cream: I like the richness of the sauce against the delicately cooked fish. I first saw edible shells being made at Geranium in Copenhagen and I loved the idea – it's a great way to serve the razor clam meat.

Serves 6

45g unsalted butter
6 pieces Cured Turbot (recipe follows)

½ recipe Artichoke Purée (recipe follows)
10g Exmoor caviar
300g Sauce Vin Blanc (recipe follows)
Dill Emulsion (page 231)
Compressed Cucumber (page 223)
6–12 pieces of sea samphire

6 Edible Razor Clam Shells (recipe follows)
1 recipe Razor Clam Tartar (recipe follows)

Put 7.5g butter on each piece of cured turbot and steam for 6 to 8 minutes depending on the thickness of the fillet.

Place a spoonful of the artichoke purée on each plate, then place a piece of steamed turbot on top. Add a little caviar and some sauce vin blanc, then garnish with dill emulsion, compressed cucumber and raw sea samphire.

Fill the edible shells with the razor clam tartar and serve alongside.

Cured Turbot

Makes 6 × 100g portions

100g sea salt
1kg water

1 fillet of turbot, skinned (about 600g after trimming)

Dissolve the salt in the water. Place the turbot fillet in the cure for 20 minutes, then remove it and place on a clean tea towel to dry in the fridge for 3 hours.

Portion the turbot into 100g pieces.

Artichoke Purée

Makes 700g

This makes more than you need, but you can freeze any excess.

500g Jerusalem artichokes, peeled
250g milk

150g cream
50g unsalted butter
hazelnut oil to taste (roughly 10ml)
salt to taste

Chop the artichokes and place in a pot with the milk. Top with a cartouche and cook on low heat until soft, then strain off the milk and place the artichokes in a blender.

Add the cream, butter and hazelnut oil and blend to a purée, then season to taste.

Sauce Vin Blanc

Makes about 700g

80g vegetable oil
100g shallots, diced
125g button mushrooms, sliced

25g unsalted butter

75g vin jaune

750g fish stock

250g cream

20g katsuobushi

3g soy lecithin
10g lemon juice
salt

We use soy lecithin here because it stabilises fats and creates a light and foamy sauce.

Heat a saucepan to medium heat and add just enough vegetable oil to cover the bottom of the pan. Sweat the shallots and mushrooms in the pan. Once they begin to start to stick to the bottom, add the butter and sweat a little further, then deglaze with the vin jaune and reduce by half.

Add the fish stock and reduce by half. Add the cream and bring to a boil. Stir in the katsuobushi and leave to infuse for 20 minutes off the heat.

Strain the sauce and, before you serve, return to a medium heat to get hot. Blend with a hand blender and add the soy lecithin while it's running: the sauce should have the constancy of double cream. Season with lemon juice and salt and keep warm until you need it.

Recipes continue on page 94

Edible Razor Clam Shells

Makes 6 shells

1 sheet feuille de brick pastry
50g vegetable oil
10g algae powder
10g charcoal powder

12 × 15cm long tube moulds

Brush a sheet of the pastry with oil, then paint it with algae and charcoal powder to make a razor clam shell effect. Cut out twelve 10 × 2cm pieces and wrap each one halfway around a 15cm long tube mould to get a half-pipe shape. Wrap neatly in greaseproof paper and place on a baking tray. You need two of these per portion to create the faux shell, so make twelve. Bake at 170°C for 6 minutes.

Razor Clam Tartar

Makes 250g

100g pomace oil
3 shallots, sliced

1kg razor clams
500g white wine

45g crème fraîche
5g dill, chopped
lemon juice
salt

Add the pomace oil to a pot on medium heat, then sweat the shallots. Once they are soft, add the razor clams and white wine and cook, covered, for 1 minute. Remove the razor clams as they open and allow them to cool.

Remove the clam meat from the shell, discarding the tough connective tissue, then cut the meat into 2mm dice.

Mix 200g of the chopped, cooked razor clams with the créme fraîche and dill and season with lemon juice and salt as necessary.

Duck Breast, Umeboshi, Beetroot, Chicory

Duck is one of my favourite meats to use in the restaurants. Roasting it whole is essential – I like the contrast of a really crispy skin that has some sweetness to it, and the soft, delicately cooked meat underneath. We get our duck from Alternative Meats, who salt-age it for 2 weeks in a Himalayan salt chamber. It is the best duck I have ever tasted by far, and I'm always stealing the off-cuts from the cooks' chopping boards when they are carving. The umeboshi plums are a fragrant addition to the plum purée we serve alongside, bringing it a unique flavour with touches of shiso and perilla.

Serves 4

1 whole Goosnargh duck, approx. 1.8kg
20g salt

....

100g vegetable oil
1 recipe Red Wine Gastrique (recipe follows)

....

10g Szechuan peppercorns, crushed
10g coriander seed, crushed
1 recipe Salt-baked Beetroot (recipe follows)
1 recipe Umeboshi Purée (page 226)
12 pieces Pickled Sliced Beetroot (page 225)
12 pieces Pickled Red Chicory (page 225)
10g cornflowers
10g butterfly sorrel

....

4 Confit Duck Bao Buns (recipe follows)

Preheat the oven to 180°C.

Take the legs off the duck by cutting behind the leg bone with a sharp knife and set them aside to use in the bao buns.

Season the duck with salt and rub thoroughly into the skin.

Heat a large pan with a little vegetable oil, then place the duck in the hot pan skin side down to begin to render the fat. You want to keep it on a medium heat and gently start to crisp up the skin, moving the duck so it gets even colour all over.

Place the duck on a roasting tray and put in the oven for 8 minutes, then turn the tray around and give it another 8 minutes. Use a meat thermometer or a cake tester to make sure the inside of the meat is nice and warm, not hot – ideally it should be around 50°C. Let the duck rest on a wire rack out of the oven and it will carry on cooking to around 58°C.

To plate, cut each roast duck breast in half diagonally, to get four triangular pieces. Place one on each plate, then brush with the gastrique and crust with the crushed Szechuan peppercorns and coriander seeds. Plate the salt-baked beets to the side, and a few dots of the umeboshi purée beside them. Roll the pickled beetroot slices into cones, and place three pieces on each plate along with three pieces of the pickled red chicory. Finish with cornflowers and sorrel and then serve with a confit duck bao bun on the side.

Red Wine Gastrique

Makes about 250g

140g sugar
180g water

100g cabernet sauvignon vinegar

In a deep pot, boil the sugar and water to get a dark caramel. Carefully deglaze with the vinegar – watch out when you add it as it will bubble up – and reduce until it is a syrupy consistency.

Store in a small tub at room temp.

Salt-baked Beetroot

Serves 4

125g T55 flour
75g fine sea salt
2g coarse sea salt
2 egg whites
1 whole egg
35g water
2 cloves, bashed into small pieces
5g milk
pinch of sugar

2 large red beetroot

10g red wine vinegar

Preheat the oven to 180°C.

Mix the T55 flour, fine and coarse salt, egg whites, whole egg, water, cloves, milk and sugar in a stand mixer for 10 to 15 minutes until you have a smooth dough.

Lay the dough out onto a tray lined with parchment paper and roll it out a little, then cut it in half. Wrap the beetroot individually in the dough, then bake for about 30 minutes or until a small knife can go in and out of the beetroot with no retention.

Crack the dough open and pull out the beetroot. Cut as you like – we cut it into cylinders with a tube cutter, then slice it on the bias. Season with a little vinegar.

Recipes continue on page 100

Confit Duck Bao Buns

Makes 14 buns

350g Brioche Dough (page 238)
14 frozen Confit Duck Balls (recipe follows)

2g Onion Salt (page 153)

We confit the duck legs, then put them in a bun to serve on the side. You can keep any surplus buns, uncooked, in the freezer.

Portion the brioche dough into fourteen 25g balls. Wrap the dough around the duck balls, pinching it tightly around them to seal. At this point you can store them in the fridge for up to 24 hours or in the freezer for a month.

Place the buns 5cm apart on a baking tray lined with parchment and cover with clingfilm. Prove for 2 to 3 hours, until the dough feels soft and springy to the touch.

Meanwhile, preheat the oven to 170°C. Remove the clingfilm from the bao buns and bake them for 6 to 8 minutes until they are very lightly golden. Allow to cool and store in the fridge until you're nearly ready to serve.

Place the cooked duck buns in a steamer for 8 minutes until they reach an internal temperature of 65°C. Sprinkle with onion salt.

Confit Duck Balls

Makes 14 balls

36g milk
36g brioche, crusts removed, chopped into a fine breadcrumb

195g Confit Duck (recipe follows)
24g reduced chicken stock
5g parsley, chopped
sherry vinegar
black pepper
salt

Warm the milk, then pour it over the brioche breadcrumbs and mix together to form a thick paste.

Fold the confit duck, reduced chicken stock and parsley into the bread paste. Season to taste with sherry vinegar, black pepper and salt, then roll the mixture into 20g balls and freeze until needed.

Confit Duck

Makes about 195g

150g fine sea salt
2 bay leaves
5g picked thyme
5g picked parsley
2.5g black peppercorns
2 star anise

2 duck legs

800g duck fat, melted

Blend the salt, bay leaves, thyme, parsley, peppercorns and star anise in a spice grinder or small food processor to form a green salt. If all the herbs do not fit, start grinding the mixture using only part of the parsley, then add more as the leaves break down. Process until well combined and a vivid green.

Rub the green salt all over the duck legs and pack in a tub for 8 hours, then thoroughly wash off the salt and pat dry.

Preheat the oven to 150°C. Place the duck legs in a deep roasting tray and cover with the melted duck fat so they're totally submerged. Cover the tray in two layers of tin foil and cook in the oven for about 2.5 hours. Leave the duck to cool in the fat, then remove and pick the meat to remove all the bone and cartilage.

polysec
FIRE
BLANKET
COMMANDER

50-day Aged Beef, Cherry Mustard, Salsify, Black Garlic

This is one of my favourite flavour combinations of all time: it was inspired by Alain Ducasse's recipe in the *Modernist Cuisine* book and has been on our menu at Aizle in some form since the beginning. The cherry mustard: it is super easy and you can keep a jar of it in the fridge for any occasion.

Serves 4

400g 50-day aged sirloin

salt
80g vegetable oil

30g cold unsalted butter, diced
2 sprigs thyme
1 garlic clove, crushed with the back of a knife

4 pieces Braised Salsify (recipe follows)
100g Black Garlic Condiment (page 226)
80g Cherry Mustard (page 227)
10g Pickled Radicchio (page 225)
5g toasted buckwheat
5g red shiso leaf

Remove the beef from the fridge 30 minutes before cooking.

Preheat the oven to 180°C. Put a heavy pan on a high heat and add a little vegetable oil. Generously salt the beef on both sides and place it in the pan, fat side down, to start to render the fat. Sear the beef until it's a nice deep, roasted colour all over, then add the butter, thyme and garlic to the pan.

Cook the beef for another 2 to 3 minutes on each side, basting as it cooks, then place in the oven for about 5 minutes.

Rest on a wire rack for at least 5 to 6 minutes before carving into four pieces.

Warm the salsify in its glaze, carefully adding a bit of water if necessary to prevent the glaze from splitting.

Place a spoonful of black garlic condiment on each plate and a quenelle of cherry mustard next to the black garlic. Place a piece of steak off-centre from the black garlic and top it with a piece of the pickled radicchio. Put a piece of salsify on the plate and top it with toasted buckwheat and some red shiso.

Braised Salsify

Serves 4

2 large sticks of salsify
20g vegetable oil

200g red wine

10g cold, unsalted butter, diced
salt
sherry vinegar

Peel the dark skin off the salsify and cut it into 6cm lengths. Roast it in a pan on a high heat with a little oil. Once coloured, deglaze with the red wine and reduce until a syrup consistency. Add the butter to finish and season with a little salt and just a few drops of sherry vinegar.

Hogget, Peas, Nori, Ewe's Curds

This is a dish I created for the Great British Menu but we have served variations of it for years. I always use hogget – lamb that is on its second spring or summer, so 1 to 2 years in age – as it has a stronger flavour than lamb but isn't as strong as mutton. It has a great texture, and for me it's the best of what we produce in Scotland.

Serves 6

1 boned hogget loin, approx. 350g

salt and pepper
100g vegetable oil

100g unsalted butter, diced
5g rosemary

100g Hogget Sauce (recipe follows)
50g Herb Emulsion (page 232)
60g Norinade (recipe follows)
6 pieces Pickled Lettuce (page 223)
100g ewe's cheese curds
4 spring onions, chopped
25g alyssum flowers
30g pea shoots
25g marigolds, tagetes or similar edible flowers

6 Pea Tarts (recipe follows)

Remove the hogget loin from the fridge 30 minutes before cooking. Heat the oven to 170°C.

Just before cooking, season the loin with salt and pepper and place skin side down in a hot pan with a little vegetable oil. On a medium heat, start to render the fat. After 5 to 6 minutes add the butter and rosemary and cook until the butter foams.

Baste the meat with the foaming butter, then place it in the oven for 6 to 8 minutes until the meat is pink, with an internal temperature of 60°C.

Remove the loin from the pan and allow to rest for 4 minutes before carving into six pieces.

To plate, place one slice of the hogget loin on the left of the plate and spoon some hogget sauce next to it. Add a small circle of herb emulsion and a teaspoon quenelle of the norinade. Place the pickled lettuce to the right, and top with a little of the cheese curds and some spring onion, alyssum, pea shoots and edible flowers. Serve the pea tart alongside.

Hogget Sauce

Makes 500g – more than you need but it keeps in the fridge.

500g lamb bones and lamb meat trimmings

85g vegetable oil
2 carrots, cut into small dice
1 onion, peeled and cut into small dice
150g button mushrooms, sliced thin

150g tomatoes, chopped
75g white wine

500g chicken stock
500g lamb stock

5g sherry vinegar
5g parsley, chopped
5g mint, chopped
salt

Heat the oven to 180°C. Roast the bones and any meat trimmings with a little oil and salt for roughly 20 to 30 minutes until nice and darkly roasted.

In a large, heavy-based pan, heat the vegetable oil, then add the carrot, onion and mushrooms. Roast them over a medium heat, and once they are coloured add the tomatoes and then deglaze with white wine. Add the roasted bones and trimmings to the pan, along with the chicken and lamb stock.

Cook out rapidly for 30 minutes, then strain and return the sauce to the pan. Reduce until it coats the back of a spoon. Season with sherry vinegar and finish with chopped parsley and mint.

Norinade

Makes 200g

180g Roscoff onion, cut into small dice
2 garlic cloves, peeled and chopped
200g pomace oil

8 sheets nori

30g dark soy
60g tosazu dashi vinegar

In a pan, cover the onions and garlic with the pomace oil. Heat until 90°C, and slowly cook until the onions are soft and translucent.

Toast the nori sheets in a dry pan for a few minutes, then add to the warm onion confit along with the dark soy and vinegar. Marinate for 30 minutes – the mix will become very soft – then chop up on a board until you have a very rough pesto consistency.

Recipes continue on page 108

Pea Tart

Makes 6 tarts

200g plain flour
20g edible charcoal powder
15g sugar
2.5g salt

100g unsalted butter

1 egg

500g fresh garden peas

60g Norinade (page 105)
100g fresh ewe's curds
5g alyssum flower

6 × 9cm tart moulds

In a stand mixer with the paddle attachment, mix the flour with the charcoal powder, sugar and salt. Add the butter and mix until it begins to look like breadcrumbs. Add the egg and, once the dough comes together, remove and briefly knead it on a table to bring it into a ball. Keep it a bit rough. Wrap in clingfilm and rest for 20 minutes.

Roll out the dough to a thickness of 2mm. Cut out six circles with a 10cm cutter and press into 9cm tart moulds. Freeze for 30 minutes.

Heat the oven to 165°C. Pierce the base of the tarts with a fork, then put another tart mould on top to keep the pastry flat and bake (from frozen) for 15 minutes.

Blanch the peas in boiling water for 3 minutes, then cool down in ice water and reserve for later.

To assemble, spoon about a teaspoon of norinade in the bottom of each tart, add some ripped up ewe's curds, and top with the peas and flowers.

Baron Bigod Custard and Lavosh Crackers

I love using Baron Bigod. It's a raw cow's milk cheese similar to a Brie De Meux but made in England. It's very nutty and has a real mushroomy, umami sort of flavour to it, but with a fairly short ageing time it is still fresh. We never do a cheese plate with chutney, grapes and biscuits at Aizle – it has always seemed boring to me – so instead we try to come up with something more contemporary, with the same amount of thought that goes in to the other dishes on the menu.

Serves 6

1 recipe Baron Bigod Custard (recipe follows)
180g Granola (recipe follows)
50g quince membrillo, cut into small cubes
10g wood sorrel

1 recipe Lavosh Crackers (recipe follows)

With a spoon, scoop the Baron Bigod custard into a quenelle and carefully place on the plate. Gently cover with about 30g of the granola, then top with small cubes of membrillo and 8 to 10 leaves of wood sorrel. Serve with the crackers.

Baron Bigod Custard

Makes 500g

150g double cream
125g milk

125g Baron Bigod, chopped

6 egg yolks

12 × 20cm ovenproof container

In a pot, bring the cream and milk to a boil. Add the cheese and, over a low heat, allow it to melt in.

Pass the mixture through a fine chinois. Once it has cooled a little, slowly beat in the eggs with a whisk. Pour into a 12 × 20cm container.

Steam at 85°C for 40 minutes until there is no wobble in the custard. We have a steamer at the restaurant but you can also bake it in a bain marie at 140°C for 40 minutes, covering it with a little clingfilm on top to make sure it steams.

Once the custard has set, leave aside to cool. If it feels a little stiff, break it up by beating with a spatula so it emulsifies, then cover with clingfilm and put in the fridge.

Recipes continue on page 111

Granola

Makes about 300g

30g vegetable oil
60g maple syrup
15g honey

200g rolled oats
10g sunflower seeds
3g salt

Heat the oven to 130°C.

Mix the oil, maple syrup and honey together a in a large bowl. Tip in the rolled oats, sunflower seeds and salt and mix well.

Tip the granola onto two baking sheets and spread it into an even layer. Bake for 15 minutes.

Scrape the cooked granola onto a flat tray to cool. It can be stored in an airtight container for up to a month.

Lavosh Crackers

Serves 4–6 plus some leftovers

4g fresh yeast
(or 2g dried active yeast)
150g milk
50g malt extract
25g sourdough starter
40g strong white flour
175g wholemeal flour

5g salt

50g vegetable oil
150g sunflower seeds

In a stand mixer with a dough hook, combine the yeast, milk, malt extract, sourdough starter, white flour and 100g of the wholemeal flour until it forms a loose dough. Cover and prove for an hour.

Add the remaining 75g wholemeal flour and the salt and mix until it comes together in a very soft, sticky dough. Tip onto a heavily floured worktop and cut into four equal-sized pieces.

Roll the dough through a pasta machine to the thinnest setting possible, flouring it as much as you need to stop it sticking. Place onto a greaseproof-lined tray and brush with oil. Season with more salt and sunflower seeds.

Bake at 170°C for 12 minutes and leave to cool, then break into pieces about the size of a credit card.

Chocolate, Amazake, Salted Milk

I usually hate chocolate with any kind of fruit but this is a rare exception as it's got just a small, subtle kick of citrus. Chocolate and miso is a combo we keep coming back to; I love the saltiness the miso brings, replacing regular salted caramel for something much more complex. We put it with amazake, a traditional Japanese drink made from koji rice that aids digestion.

Serve 6

1 recipe Chocolate Mousse with Miso Crème Centre (recipe follows)
1 recipe White Chocolate Spray (recipe follows)

....

1 recipe Kataifi Nests (recipe follows)
1 recipe Calamansi Gel (recipe follows)
½ recipe Chocolate Tuille (recipe follows)
10g micro corn shoots

....

½ recipe Salted Milk Ice Cream (recipe follows)

Place the mousses, direct from the freezer, onto a tray and spritz with white chocolate spray until they are completely white. Leave for 2 hours to defrost.

Once defrosted, gently transfer one mousse to each plate. Top with a kataifi nest, and dot with calamansi gel, pieces of chocolate tuille and a few micro corn shoots.

Serve with a quenelle of salted milk ice cream on the side.

Recipes continue on page 114

Chocolate Mousse with Miso Crème Centre

Makes 6 (and you might have a small bowl left over)

100g dark chocolate, roughly chopped

215g double cream

1 gold gelatine leaf

40g egg yolk
1 whole egg
67g sugar

6 pieces frozen Miso Crème (recipe follows)

6 × 6cm spherical silicone moulds

These can be kept in the freezer for up to a month. Remove from the freezer 2 hours before serving (5 hours if you're defrosting them in the fridge).

Melt the chocolate in a bain marie. In a bowl, whip the cream to ribbon stage.

In another bowl, soak the gelatine in cold water until soft.

Combine the egg yolk, whole egg and sugar and cook in a bain marie, whisking all the time, to make a sabayon. Take it to 50°C, then add in the melted chocolate, then the squeezed-out gelatine leaf and whisk until everything is combined and the gelatine has dissolved. Take the bowl off the heat and fold in the whipped cream. Transfer to a piping bag.

Pipe the chocolate mousse into the moulds, filling them half full. Tap the moulds on your work surface to remove any air bubbles, then place one frozen miso crème in the centre of each mould. Fill with the remaining chocolate mousse, tap the moulds again and then smooth the tops with a palette knife so they are level.

Freeze and use within a month.

Miso Crème

Makes about 18 balls. Any leftovers can be kept in the freezer

1 gold gelatine leaf

270g double cream
100g milk
65g amazake
40g miso

salt

18 × 2cm spherical silicone moulds

Soak the gelatine in cold water until soft.

In a pot, combine the cream, milk, amazake and miso and warm up on a low heat. Add the softened gelatine and season with salt to taste.

Pour into the moulds, allow to cool and then freeze. When hard, un-mould and store in the freezer until needed.

White Chocolate Spray

Makes 120g

100g white chocolate
20g cocoa butter

chocolate spray gun

Melt the chocolate and cocoa butter together in a bain marie and place into the chocolate spray gun.

Kataifi Nests

Makes 6

180g kataifi pastry
20g icing sugar

Preheat the oven to 180°C.

Unfold the kataifi pastry, then lightly dust it in icing sugar. Separate into six pieces and shape into nests by wrapping each piece tightly around the back of a small mould or egg cup. Place on a baking tray and bake for 5 minutes until just golden.

Calamansi Gel

Makes 140g

50g calamansi juice
75g apple juice
15g sugar

1.4–7g ultratex (1–5% of the liquid's weight)

Calamansi lime is from the Philippines; it's similar to yuzu (but cheaper!).

Combine the calamansi juice with the apple juice and sugar. Whisk in the ultratex bit by bit until the juice thickens to the gel consistency.

Chocolate Tuille

Makes 135g

50g fondant
50g isomalt
50g glucose

35g white chocolate, chopped

Heat the fondant, isomalt and glucose to 150°C, stirring regularly. Add the chocolate and pour onto a silicone mat.

Let the mixture cool a little, then pull off little pieces and stretch them as thin as you can.

Salted Milk Ice Cream

Makes about 750g

100g egg yolks
100g sugar
30g milk powder

500g milk
75g double cream
20g invert sugar
20g glucose

5g sea salt

ice cream maker

In a bowl, mix the egg yolks, sugar and milk powder together.

Warm the milk, cream, invert sugar and glucose in a pot until steaming. Slowly pour the hot milk onto the egg yolk mix, whisking all the time, then return to the pot and cook out, stirring, until it reaches 80°C. Add sea salt to taste.

Leave the mix to cool, then chill and churn. Freeze for about 30 minutes before making quenelles.

Rhubarb and Custard

Inspired by one of my favourite childhood dessert combinations, the rhubarb and custard we serve at Aizle is a very simple dish but one that uses a lot of technique. Growing up, my mum always had garden rhubarb growing, which is greener and much more sour than the fabulous forced rhubarb we get from Yorkshire at the start of every year. She would make rhubarb crumble with custard, so in the restaurant we give the custard the texture of 'crumble' by spraying it into liquid nitrogen.

Serves 6

1 recipe Rhubarb Sorbet (recipe follows)
½ recipe Rhubarb Compote (recipe follows)
1 recipe Anglaise Snow (recipe follows)
6 pieces of Rhubarb Glass (recipe follows)

Spoon some rhubarb sorbet into a bowl. Top with rhubarb compote and surround by anglaise snow. Finish with a piece of rhubarb glass on the top.

Recipes continue on page 118

Rhubarb Sorbet

Makes 700g

190g sugar
3g locust bean gum

500g Rhubarb Purée (recipe follows)
citric acid to taste

ice cream machine

Whisk together the sugar and locust bean gum. In a large pot, bring the rhubarb purée to the boil and add in the sugar mixture. Continue to boil for 30 seconds, then remove from the heat. Cool, then season with citric acid. Refrigerate for at least 2 hours before churning.

Rhubarb Purée

Makes about 700g

500g forced rhubarb, chopped into small pieces
90g grenadine
150g cold water

Place the rhubarb, grenadine and water in a deep pot and gently poach on a medium heat until very soft. Blend into a smooth purée – it should be a soup-like consistency.

Rhubarb Compote

Makes 600g

250g sugar
500g water
100g grenadine

500g forced rhubarb, trimmed into 8cm pieces

1–5g ultratex to thicken (usually 1–5% of the liquid's weight)

This makes more than you will need but it will keep in the fridge for a few days.

Bring the sugar, water and grenadine to a boil and reduce to a gentle simmer.

Add the rhubarb and poach until it is just soft but still has a slight bite, about 2 to 3 minutes. With a slotted spoon, remove the rhubarb from the liquid and allow to cool.

Thicken 100g of the reserved poaching liquid with enough ultratex to give you a nice glossy gel.

Dice the rhubarb and fold into the thickened juice. It should have a jammy consistency.

Anglaise Snow

Fills 1 iSi siphon gun

230g milk
120g double cream
1 vanilla pod

90g egg yolk
100g sugar

2 gold gelatine leaves

In a pot, heat the milk, cream and vanilla together until scalding.

In a bowl, whisk the egg yolks with the sugar. In another bowl, soak the gelatine leaves in cold water until they are soft.

Temper the hot milk mixture into the eggs, slowly pouring it in while whisking all the time, then return the mix to the pot and cook until it reaches 84°C. Remove the vanilla pod. Squeeze the excess water off the gelatine leaves, then add them to the custard and stir until they have fully dissolved.

Place the anglaise in an iSi siphon gun and charge with two N_2O canisters. In the restaurant we spray the espuma into liquid nitrogen and then crush it with a whisk to make a snow, but at home you can use as is.

Rhubarb Glass

Makes 6 pieces

195g Rhubarb Purée (page 118)
33g isomalt
28g icing sugar
7g glucose

In a pan, heat the rhubarb purée with the isomalt, icing sugar and glucose until the sugars are dissolved.

Thinly spread onto silicone mats and dehydrate at 70°C for 10 hours until hard. You can't really get the same results without a dehydrator.

Break or cut into pieces.

Sea Buckthorn Posset, Yoghurt, Carrot, Walnut

My former sous chef Matt Smith and I dreamt this one up at the original Aizle. Sea Buckthorn grows around the coast of Scotland – we pick ours from Gullane, just down the Firth of Forth from Edinburgh. It is harvested late autumn and is very acidic, so perfect for making posset.

Serves 6

1 recipe Sea Buckthorn Posset (recipe follows)

....

6 pieces Isomalt Tuille (recipe follows)
1 recipe Candied Walnuts (recipe follows)
100g Carrot Purée (recipe follows)
1 recipe Yoghurt Sorbet (recipe follows)
lemon balm
frozen sea buckthorn berries

Place a posset on each plate direct from the freezer and leave for 30 minutes to come to room temperature.

Balance a piece of isomalt tuille on top, then add some of the crumbled candied walnuts, a few dots of carrot purée and a spoonful of yoghurt sorbet. We finish it with lemon balm and a few frozen berries of sea buckthorn.

Recipes continue on page 122

Sea Buckthorn Posset

Makes 6

500g double cream
90g caster sugar

200g fresh sea buckthorn juice, reduced to 100g

6 × 6cm circular silicone moulds

Put the double cream in a large pan with the sugar. Bring slowly to the boil and simmer for 3 minutes. Take it off the heat, add the reduced sea buckthorn juice and whisk well.

Pour into the moulds and freeze overnight – this will allow you to turn them out cleanly.

Isomalt Tuille

Makes 200g

100g glucose
100g isomalt

Bring the glucose and isomalt together in a medium pot and cook until they reach 160°C on a sugar thermometer. Pour onto a non-stick silicon mat and leave to cool.

Once cool, break into pieces and blend into a fine powder. Sprinkle the powder onto a non-stick silicon mat using a fine sieve so you get a thin, even layer.

Bake in the oven at 160°C until the powder has melted, and then leave to cool. You will have a clear sugar-glass-type tuille to shape or cut to size as you like.

Candied Walnuts

Makes 200g

125g walnut halves

100g caster sugar
3g ground cinnamon
0.6g salt
45g milk

Heat the oven to 180°C.

Roast the nuts in a single layer on a tray for about 10 minutes until golden.

Place the sugar, cinnamon, salt and milk in a pan and cook out until the mix reaches 113°C on a digital thermometer – it will look clear but thickened. Add the walnuts and stir well so they are all coated evenly.

Tip the nuts onto baking paper and leave until they are hard and cool. Hand chop into a small crumble.

Carrot Purée

Makes 250g

250g carrots

150g carrot juice
50g sugar
5g salt

0.5g xanthan gum

Peel and chop the carrots into small dice and place in a vacuum bag with the carrot juice, sugar and salt. Seal the bag and steam at 90°C for 45 minutes until the carrots are very soft.

Empty the contents of the bag into a Thermomix or high-powered blender with the xanthan gum, and blend until smooth. Check the seasoning – it should be sweet so adjust if need be with a little more sugar.

Yoghurt Sorbet

Makes about 600g

500g yoghurt

70g sugar
65g liquid glucose
20g invert sugar

In a pot, warm the yoghurt, then add the sugar, glucose and invert sugar and cook to 65°C. Once cool, chill in the fridge, then churn in an ice cream machine. Freeze for 30 minutes, then quenelle to serve.

Noto

Noto is my small-plates, NYC/Japanese-inspired restaurant. It was named after a very good friend of mine, Bob Noto, my 80-year-old flatmate when I first moved to NYC, and it is heavily inspired by the cool, low-key restaurants I used to love when I lived there. The idea was simple: a small restaurant with a busy bar that you can eat or just drink at, with great food at a price point accessible to all, soundtracked by my favourite hip hop. The recipes here are casual but still refined, and they're made for sharing.

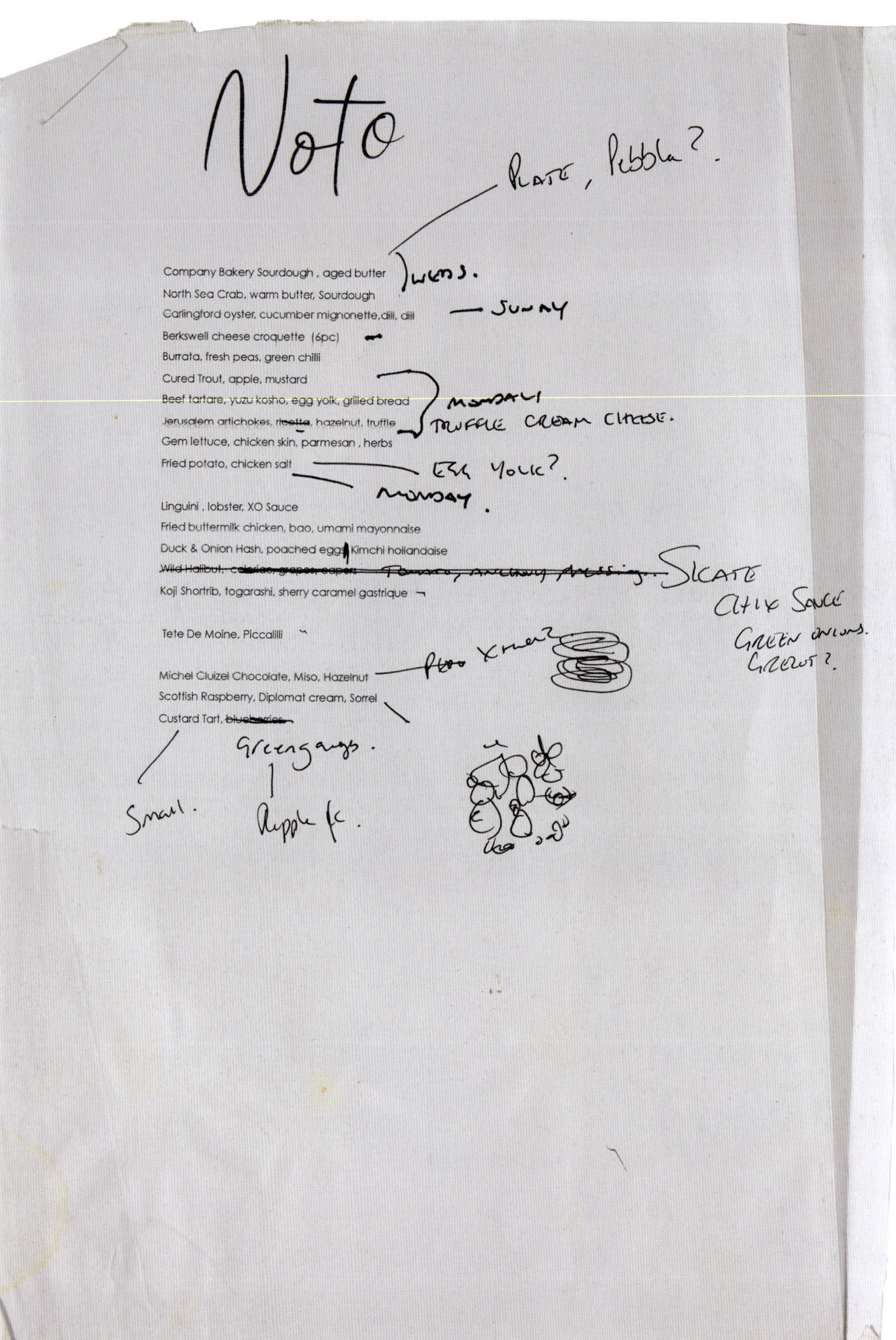

Noto

Company Bakery Sourdough , aged butter
North Sea Crab, warm butter, Sourdough
Carlingford oyster, cucumber mignonette,dill, dill
Berkswell cheese croquette (6pc)
Burrata, fresh peas, green chilli
Cured Trout, apple, mustard
Beef tartare, yuzu kosho, egg yolk, grilled bread
Jerusalem artichokes, ~~ricotta~~, hazelnut, truffle
Gem lettuce, chicken skin, parmesan , herbs
Fried potato, chicken salt

Linguini , lobster, XO Sauce
Fried buttermilk chicken, bao, umami mayonnaise
Duck & Onion Hash, poached eggs, Kimchi hollandaise
~~Wild Halibut, celeriac, grapes, capers~~
Koji Shortrib, togarashi, sherry caramel gastrique

Tete De Moine, Piccalilli

Michel Cluizel Chocolate, Miso, Hazelnut
Scottish Raspberry, Diplomat cream, Sorrel
Custard Tart, ~~blueberries~~

Edinburgh
2014–2019

Very early into opening Aizle, Krystal got pregnant. I was super happy: I had always wanted kids, I felt like I was getting everything I ever wanted. When she went on maternity leave, we employed Jade as a restaurant manager. It was meant to be a temporary thing – we assumed Krystal would come back – but Jade was doing an amazing job and in the end Krystal went on to pursue her own dream of being a full-time comedian. Ever since, Jade has played a huge role in what we've achieved and where we'll go next. She's always been a good barometer for how far to push things and how customers perceive what we do. She is now Operations Manager but in a lot of ways she is so much more: she cares for the businesses as her own, and has always got my back; you need people like that in your camp and I'm grateful to her for everything.

In 2019 we found another great venue on Thistle Street, a cobbled lane filled with independent businesses right in the centre of Edinburgh. Krystal, Jade and I visited the site a couple of times, and they weren't really into it, but I thought it had potential and sitting in the empty restaurant I felt good about it. Instinct is important to trust; restaurants have personality, and you need to have vision for them.

We did the deal, got the keys and started dreaming up Noto. I must add at this point we had no real capital to expand, we had no right really to do it, but if you want it badly enough you can work around all that. The bank was keen to lend again so we took a chunky loan from them and a little loan from Aizle, we put most of the equipment on finance and we got stuck in. It cost us about £150,000 to open: we refurbed in 8 weeks and opened in the second week of the Edinburgh Fringe.

People said I was mental to open a restaurant in the Fringe but, again, I looked at it differently. There were going be lots of tourists in town and plenty of people out looking to eat and spend money; we just had to guide them in and we would have a great start. It took off right away, and a lot of good faith in Aizle followed us to Noto.

I always wanted a more casual offering to Aizle, as that's generally how I enjoy eating – delicious food and not too spendy. Noto earned a Michelin Bib Gourmand in its first few months of opening; better than that, it's been busy since day one.

Opposite: The very first Noto menu with scribbled notes as we cooked our way through it.

Noto
MICHELIN
2021

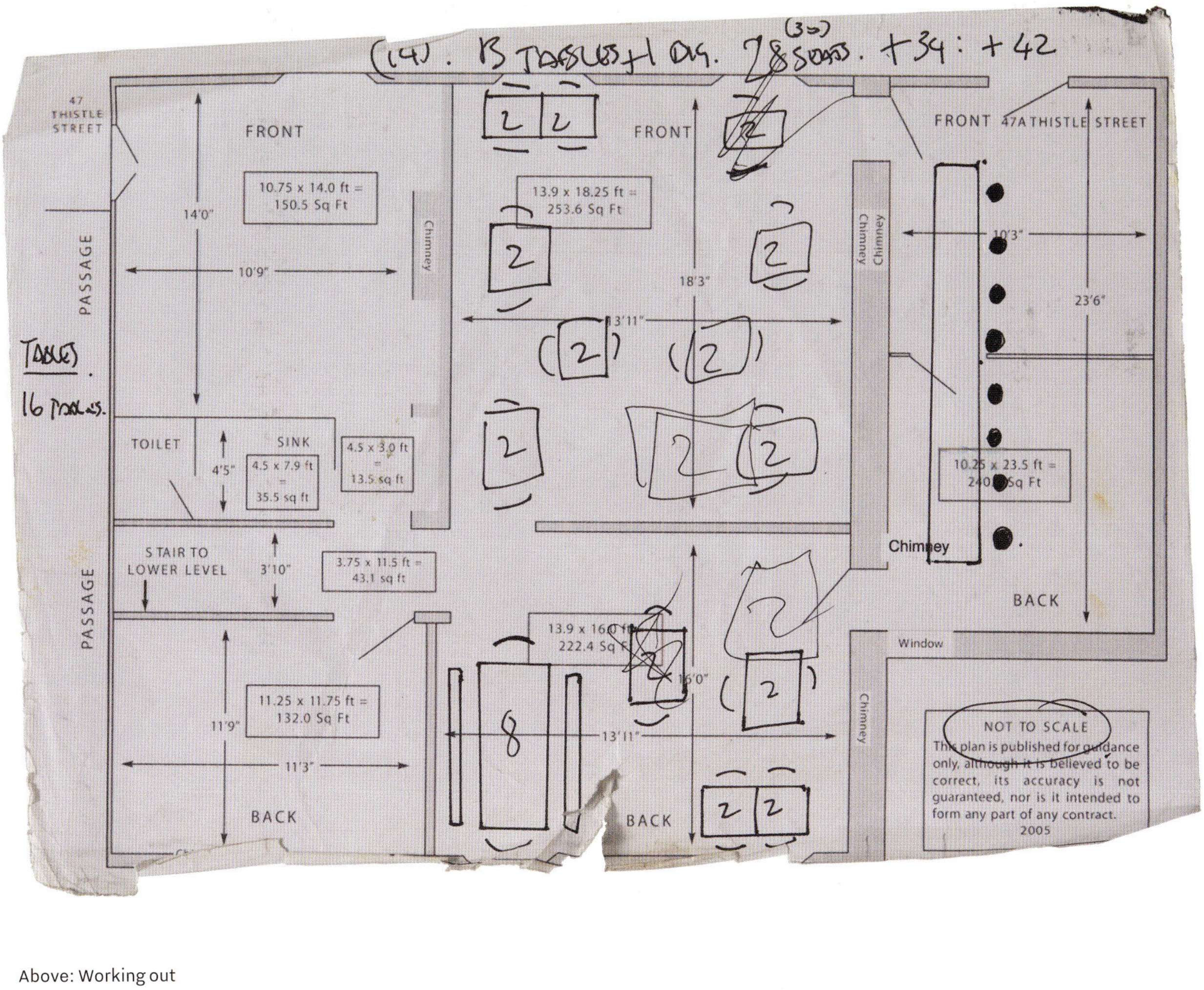

Above: Working out how to fit the tables in.

Noto the Man

Bob Noto was a sweet old man who always dressed smartly. He wore Nike Air trainers for his walks and trendy-before-they-were-trendy, thick, black-rimmed glasses. He was in his eighties and was a true New Yorker: he'd lived there his whole life and knew the city inside out. He ran his one-bedroom apartment on West 69th between Broadway and Columbus Avenue as a B&B, and he took pity on me. The deal was that I could sleep in the main bedroom when there wasn't anyone booked in, and when he had guests I could sleep with him in the attic. Imagine a massive kitchen-living room with a small mezzanine area above the kitchen – this was the 'attic'. Bob and I would sleep up there, him on one side of a small wooden partition and me on the other, whilst our guest slept in the nice, cosy room below us.

I should mention that Bob also wore an oxygen mask as his health wasn't the best, so this pumped away through the night. It was an unusual arrangement to say the least, but I went with it and met a lot of interesting people, as his guests tended to be creative types, solo travellers and wannabe artists. Bob and I would often have dinner together since I didn't know many people. He would tell me stories about his life in NYC: the celebrities he'd met, the parties he'd been to back in the city's heyday. It was fascinating. I would go grocery shopping at Fairways or Zabar's, massive food emporiums that sold amazing produce at reasonable prices. I would buy rotisserie chickens, Caesar salads, fresh sourdough and good butter and take it back to the apartment to eat. We spent many a day chatting over a roast chicken dinner. He took me to some great sushi and dim sum spots, as well as to New Year's parties with friends of his who always made me feel welcome.

Sadly, as Bob got older and his health deteriorated, it became an unmanageable living situation so I left and moved to Queens with three cooks from work. But I always regretted not having been of more support to Bob in those last days, and I named my second restaurant after him to honour the man who had made such an impression on me. After Noto had been open a few years, Bob's family contacted me and we managed to meet for dinner there and exchange stories about the caring and funny man we had known. Today, there's a plaque in his honour outside his old house. He wasn't Bill Gates and he never played for the Yankees, but he has a plaque in his honour on a street in NYC. That's when you know you're a legend.

Opposite: Bob Noto. The ladder up to the little shelf where we both slept is on the right.

Potato Dauphine, Miso Mustard Mayo

This is a great bar snack to get stuck into when you're drinking at Noto. Fried potato in any form sells: fact. I learnt how to make dauphine potatoes when I was 14, as my dad used to serve them with beef as a side. This version is more Asian in essence than classic French but the technique is the same. Seasoning the potatoes with dashi stock powder really is the game changer – the seaweed umami flavour just makes you want to keep coming back for more.

Serves 6 as a snack (5 pieces each)

1 recipe Potato Dauphine (recipe follows)

½ recipe Miso Mustard Mayo (page 235)
1 recipe Puffed Potato (recipe follows)
1 recipe Furikake (recipe follows)

vegetable oil to deep fry

Deep fry the dauphine at 180°C for 3 to 4 minutes, until they float to the top of the oil. Drain them on paper towels and plate up, topped with miso mayo and some puffed potato and furikake.

Recipes continue on page 134

Potato Dauphine

Makes 30

2 large Rooster potatoes
salt

95g water
95g milk
75g unsalted butter
2.5g sugar
5g salt
7g dashi powder

95g flour

2 large eggs

Preheat the oven to 180°C. Place the potatoes on a salt-lined tray, prick each one several times and bake for 60 to 90 minutes until cooked.

While they're still hot, cut the potatoes in half and scoop out the centres. Pass through a ricer and weigh out 120g of the mash. This can all be done a day in advance.

To make the dauphine, place the water, milk, butter, sugar, salt and dashi powder in a medium pot and put over a medium heat until the butter melts and the liquid comes to a simmer. Add the flour and mix aggressively, then reduce the heat and continue to cook, beating, until the dough is tight and glossy.

Place the dough in a stand mixer with the paddle attachment and turn on to medium speed. Add the eggs one at a time, making sure the first one is completely incorporated before adding the next. Stop the mixer and reduce the speed to low. Add the reserved 120g cooked potato and gently mix until it begins to combine. Adjust the seasoning, and fold in by hand to ensure it is evenly combined.

Transfer the dough to a well-greased container. Cover the surface directly with clingfilm and refrigerate for 2 hours.

Weigh the dough into 20g portions, then roll them into balls. Put the balls onto a baking tray sprayed with oil, then lightly spray the balls themselves before placing in the fridge or freezer. They will keep for 2 days in the fridge, or 2 weeks in the freezer – defrost them for an hour before using.

Puffed Potato

Makes 20g

20g Sosa Air Bag potato granules

salt

vegetable oil to deep fry

Deep fry the dried potato at 200°C for 2 minutes, until they float to the top of the oil and puff up.

Drain on paper towels and season with a little salt.

Furikake

Makes 35g

20g mixed sesame seeds, toasted
10g rice seasoning powder, crushed
5g kombu flakes, crushed

In a small bowl, mix the sesame seeds, rice seasoning and kombu flakes together.

Noto
Please ring door bell for deliveries
IF NO ANSWER LEAVE GOODS AT DOOR

Crab Butter

The signature dish of Noto, and definitely the most simple thing we have ever served, I could eat this forever. When I am really hungry I crave it: pure seafood indulgence from a humble ingredient, affordable but very luxurious at the same time.

Serves 1–2

30g Picked Crabmeat (recipe follows)
35g cultured butter
35g unsalted butter
10g water

salt
2–3 drops lemon juice

Dill Oil (page 231)
3g dill, chopped
3g chives, chopped
5g dried kombu flakes

In a small pot, gently warm the crab with the cultured and unsalted butters and the water (which helps it emulsify). Take care not to split the butter with excessive heat. Season with salt and lemon juice as necessary.

At Noto we serve our crab in a cleaned head sitting on a mound of wet salt but it is just as tasty served in a ramekin. Either way, top the crab butter with a drizzle of dill oil and the chopped dill and chives and finish with the kombu flakes.

Picked Crabmeat

Yields about 200g

1 live crab

Cook the crab in boiling salted water for 8 minutes per kg, then remove it from the water and allow to cool on a tray. I prefer not to ice crabs, but it's important to refrigerate it once it's cooled down, ideally within 30 minutes.

Crack the crab shell and remove all the white meat from the claws, legs and head. Pick over the meat three times to ensure no shell or cartilage is remaining, then keep it in the fridge and use within a couple of days.

If you're using the crab head to serve the crab butter in, remove any internal parts or membranes and scrub it clean. Boil it in vinegared water for a minute, then rinse and trim the outer edge of the shell with sharp scissors.

Cured Trout, Ponzu, Cucumber, Kohlrabi

Sea trout is a great alternative to salmon; it is very fatty and has a good oil content. It's the same species as brown trout: all trout hatch in fresh water but some migrate to the sea where they get a much richer source of food. The ponzu really makes this, so be sure to flood the plate.

Serves 4

24 pieces Cured Trout (recipe follows)
20g Lovage Emulsion (page 232)
20g Tomato Ponzu Fluid Gel (recipe follows)
¼ recipe Compressed Cucumber and Kohlrabi (page 223)
75g Ponzu Base (recipe follows)
20g Dill Oil (page 231)
5g chives, chopped into batons
5g dill, picked

Place six pieces of trout on each plate, then add three large dots of lovage emulsion and four small dots of tomato ponzu fluid gel. Add some pieces of compressed cucumber and kohlrabi. Flood the plate with the ponzu base and drizzle with dill oil before garnishing with chive batons and picked dill.

Cured Trout

Makes 1kg

1kg Loch Etive sea trout fillet

100g brown sugar
100g salt

150g white wine

2 sheets nori, blended into a powder

This recipe makes more than you need but you can keep it in the freezer and defrost it as you need it. Ask your fishmonger to pin bone and skin the sea trout for you.

Trim, pin bone and skin the trout if it hasn't been done. Mix the sugar and salt and coat the sides of the trout evenly. Place the trout on a large piece of clingfilm. Pour over the white wine and wrap into a parcel. Cure in the fridge for 6 hours.

Gently wash the trout and pat dry. Cover it in nori powder, then wrap tightly in clingfilm and freeze until needed.

To portion, remove the fish from the freezer and allow to defrost slightly. Slice into 1cm thick pieces, allowing six pieces per portion, then keep in the fridge until needed.

Recipes continue on page 140

Tomato Ponzu Fluid Gel

Makes 225g

163g Ponzu Base (recipe follows)
63g tomato juice
4.5g agar agar

In a pot, mix the ponzu base, tomato juice and agar agar and allow to rest for 15 minutes. Heat to a simmer for 5 minutes, whisking often. Allow the gel to set completely before blending, then pass through a sieve and season.

Ponzu Base

Makes 240g

120g rice wine vinegar
60g lime juice
30g soy sauce
30g sugar

1 piece kombu

Mix the rice wine vinegar, lime juice, soy sauce and sugar together. In a dry pan, toast the kombu until it is a little smoky, then place it in a jar and pour over the liquid. Store in the fridge and strain before use.

Beef Tartar, Black Garlic, Jerusalem Artichoke

We have never taken beef tartar off the menu since we opened Noto. My advice is to buy the best beef you can, ideally from a trusted local butcher – either grass-fed or organic, something with some nice marbling. I find the rump a great cut for this as it's not too expensive.

Serves 4

1 recipe Beef Tartar (recipe follows)
10g capers, chopped
10g cornichons, chopped
2g parsley, chopped
2 egg yolks
Tabasco sauce
L&P Worcestershire sauce
salt

....

50g Beef Fat Mayo (page 233)
50g Black Garlic Condiment (page 226)
Pickled Shimeji Mushrooms (page 222)
1 recipe J-choke Chips (recipe follows)
10g baby watercress, picked nasturtiums

Mix the beef with the capers, cornichons, parsley, egg yolks, Tabasco and L&P. Check seasoning and adjust to taste.

Spoon the beef tartar mix neatly onto each plate. Top with dots of beef fat mayo and black garlic condiment. Add a few pickled shimeji mushrooms and J-choke chips, then finish with baby watercress and nasturtiums.

Recipes continue on page 145

i've got you

Beef Tartar

Serves 4

400g beef rump steak

5g vegetable oil

Clean the beef, removing any excess fat and sinew. In an extremely hot pan, add a little vegetable oil, then sear the beef on all sides. Allow it to cool on a resting rack.

Trim off and discard the seared edges of beef, then slice it into 3mm strips. Layer the strips between sheets of parchment paper and freeze.

To serve, remove the beef from the freezer and finely dice it. Store on top of ice until you are ready to serve.

J-choke Chips

Serves 4

2 Jerusalem artichokes

salt

vegetable oil to deep fry

Slice the j-chokes to 1mm thick on a mandolin, and then immediately deep fry at 140°C until golden brown. Lightly season with salt and drain on paper towels.

Burrata, Romesco, Red Chilli

According to Jade Johnston, our Ops Manager and partner in everything we do, burrata is hands down the best cheese in the world. It is super versatile, great for sharing and easy to source. It's also delicious paired with my ride-or-die sauce, romesco. We use a little gochujang chilli paste to give the romesco a slight change of direction from its native Spanish roots.

Serves 2 with plenty of sauce

1 burrata

1 recipe Romesco (recipe follows)
1 red chilli, sliced
10g olive oil
sea salt
black pepper

Place the burrata onto a paper towel to drain any excess liquid. Spoon plenty of romesco onto a plate and put the burrata on top. Add a couple of slices of red chilli, season with a little sea salt and cracked black pepper and then drizzle over the olive oil. Serve with toasted focaccia (page 239).

Romesco

Makes about 650g

75g flaked almonds, toasted
75g whole hazelnuts, toasted

250g shop-bought roasted peppers, drained and seeds removed
250g tinned tomatoes, drained overnight

30–60g gochujang chilli paste, depending on desired spiciness
45g olive oil
8 garlic cloves, finely grated
10g sherry vinegar
5g smoked paprika
8g salt
sugar to taste

Pulse the almonds and hazelnuts together in a food processor to form coarse crumbs, then place in a large bowl.

Blend the roasted peppers and drained tomatoes together in the food processor until incorporated but not smooth. Add to the toasted nuts.

Blend the gochujang, olive oil, garlic, sherry vinegar, smoked paprika and salt to form a paste. Add this to the nut mixture and season as necessary with more salt, sugar and vinegar.

Prawn Toast

Traditionally a Cantonese dim sum snack created in Hong Kong, the Noto version of this takeaway classic has a thick, distinguishable layer of moussey prawn paste, so you can really see it. I love prawn toast, and it's very simple to prepare.

Serves 4

4 slices Pain de Mie (page 240)
10g sesame oil
1 recipe Prawn Paste (recipe follows)
100g sesame seeds

50g Bulldog tonkatsu sauce
50g Kewpie Mayo (page 233)
4 spring onions, sliced
katsuobushi flakes

vegetable oil to deep fry

Brush the bread slices on one side with sesame oil, then spread a thick layer of the prawn paste on top and coat generously in sesame seeds.

Deep fry at 180°C for 4 minutes until golden brown on all sides – the internal temperature should be above 65°C. Cut each slice into four.

Top with tonkatsu sauce and pipe over some zigzags of kewpie mayo. Finish with a few sliced spring onions and a scatter of katsuobushi flakes.

Prawn Paste

Makes about 300g

250g raw prawns, chopped
8g ginger, chopped
1 garlic clove, chopped
2 spring onions, sliced

45g egg whites

7g salt

In a blender, pulse the prawns with the ginger, garlic and spring onion to form a paste. Add the egg whites and blend until combined, then lightly season with the salt. Store over ice when not in use.

Chicken Katsu Sandwich

Sandwiches, a British staple, perfected by the Japanese! We make the bread for this, which makes all the difference: it's a chunky sandwich so it needs a decent white pan loaf, and a soft milk bread like pain de mie is ideal. Tonkatsu, or Bulldog sauce, is a Japanese condiment similar to a BBQ sauce, with a very tangy, sour, dark molasses flavour. It is readily available in most Asian supermarkets.

Serves 4

8 thick slices Pain de Mie (page 240)

100g white cabbage, shredded
100g Kimchi (page 192)
150g Kewpie Mayo (page 233)

2 × recipe Buttermilk Fried Chicken using 8 boneless chicken thighs (page 41)
100g Bulldog tonkatsu sauce

Toast the bread until golden brown.

Mix the cabbage and kimchi with 50g kewpie mayo and season as necessary. Spread the remaining mayonnaise thinly on all eight slices of toasted bread, then cover four of them evenly with the kimchi mix. Place two pieces of chicken on top of the kimchi mix and drizzle with tonkatsu sauce.

Cover with the remaining four slices and gently press down. Slice off the crusts and cut the sandwiches in half.

Chicken Bao Buns

We first did these at Aizle 1.0. We used to make them every day and, due to the unpredictable nature of guessing how many covers we would do each night, there were always leftovers. So, after service we would put them up for the staff to snack on and I'm sure it kept some of them with us for longer than they would have been otherwise as they were hooked. I know one ex-member of staff who has used this recipe extensively at his own restaurant.

Serves 10

500g Brioche Dough (page 238)
20 frozen Confit Chicken Balls (recipe follows)

....

100g Onion Mayo (page 234)
50g Onion Salt (recipe follows)
4 spring onions, sliced
1 recipe Crispy Chicken Skin (recipe follows)

Portion the brioche dough into twenty 25g balls. Wrap the dough around the chicken balls, pinching it tightly around them to seal. At this point you can store them in the fridge for up to 24 hours or in the freezer for a month.

Place the buns 5cm apart on a baking tray lined with parchment and cover with clingfilm. Prove for 2 to 3 hours, until the dough feels soft and springy to the touch.

Meanwhile, preheat the oven to 170°C. Remove the clingfilm from the bao buns and bake them for 6 to 8 minutes until they are very lightly golden. Allow to cool and then store in the fridge.

Place the cooked chicken buns in a steamer for 8 minutes until they reach an internal temperature of 65°C. Top with onion mayo, onion salt, spring onion and crispy chicken skin.

Confit Chicken Balls

Makes 26 balls

75g brioche, crusts removed
75g milk

....

375g Confit Chicken Leg (recipe follows)
50g reduced chicken stock
10g parsley, chopped

....

sherry vinegar
salt and pepper

Chop the brioche into a fine breadcrumb. Warm the milk, then pour it over the brioche breadcrumbs and mix together to form a thick paste.

Fold the confit chicken, reduced chicken stock and parsley into the bread paste. Season to taste with sherry vinegar, salt and black pepper, then roll the mixture into 20g balls and freeze until needed.

Confit Chicken Leg

Makes about 375g

100g salt
1 bay leaf
2.5g picked thyme
5g picked parsley
2.5g ground black pepper
1 star anise

4 chicken legs

800g duck fat or vegetable oil

Blend the salt, bay leaf, thyme, parsley, black pepper and star anise in a food processor to form a green salt. Rub the chicken legs in the salt and allow to cure for 5 hours, then wash the cure off and pat dry.

Place the chicken legs in a deep pot and cover with duck fat (or vegetable oil). Ensure the legs are submerged and top with a parchment cartouche.

Heat the pot gently on the stovetop until the fat has warmed evenly, then allow to cook on a medium–low heat for 2.5 to 3 hours until the meat becomes tender and falls off the bone.

Remove the pot from the heat and allow to rest for 30 minutes. Take the legs out of the fat and rest until the meat is cool enough to be picked. Carefully pick the meat to remove all the bone and cartilage, and reserve all the chicken skin.

Strain the fat, discarding all the chicken residue, then let it cool and store in the fridge for reuse.

Onion Salt

Makes more than you need but it keeps forever in an airtight jar

6 large white onions, finely chopped
gluten-free flour

Maldon salt
50-80g maltodextrin

vegetable oil to deep fry

Dredge the onions in flour and then deep fry, in batches, at 200°C until they're black.

Put the fried onions on a tray and dehydrate overnight at 70°C.

In a food processor, lightly pulse the dried onions, then weigh them and add 10% of the weight in salt. Mix well and add enough maltodextrin to make a dry sand mixture.

Crispy Chicken Skin

Preheat the oven to 180°C.

Take all the reserved chicken skin from the confit chicken and place it flat on baking trays lined with baking parchment. Bake in the oven for 20 minutes, then carefully drain the excess fat from the trays and return the skin to the oven until it is crispy. Place on paper towels to drain any remaining fat and allow to cool.

Jerusalem Artichoke, Cheddar, Maple

Jerusalem artichokes have an earthy, slightly sweet flavour and a texture not dissimilar to potato, so we often use them in similar ways. This is a take on the American twice-baked potato, where you mix the scooped out potato mash with cheese and put it back into the fried potato shell. Weirdly it was never a great seller at Noto, but it should have been and I love it so it's getting a second chance here.

Serves 4

1 recipe Jerusalem Artichoke Shells and reserved artichoke flesh (recipe follows)
50ml double cream
salt
5g chives, chopped

50g Cheddar Custard (recipe follows)
1 recipe Maple Glaze (recipe follows)
100g watercress or pea shoots
Basic Vinaigrette (page 235)

Warm the reserved scooped out insides of the artichokes in a medium-sized pot with the cream. Season with a little salt and finish by adding the chives. Spoon the mixture back into the crispy artichoke shells.

Arrange three artichokes to a plate, then top with dots of Cheddar custard. Drizzle with a little of the maple glaze. Dress the top with watercress or pea shoots that have a little vinaigrette on them. We sometimes finish this dish with shaved fresh truffles or pickled onions with pickled mustard seeds.

Jerusalem Artichoke Shells

Makes 12

6 large Jerusalem artichokes, washed
2 garlic bulbs, split into cloves
30g thyme
salt

vegetable oil for deep frying

Place the j-chokes in a medium-sized pot with plenty of cold water. Season with salt and add the garlic and thyme. Bring to a boil and simmer until tender, about 20 minutes.

Drain the j-chokes and allow them to cool slightly. Slice them in half and scoop out the soft flesh with a spoon, being careful to keep the skin intact. Reserve the artichoke flesh for later.

Dehydrate the skins at 60°C overnight until completely dry, then deep fry them at 180°C for 3 to 4 minutes until they are golden and crispy. Season with a little salt and set aside.

Recipes continue on page 158

Cheddar Custard

Makes 800g

This makes more than you need, but it's impossible to make in smaller quantities.

200g milk
200g water
300g Cheddar, diced
(discard any rind)
8 eggs
6g agar agar

salt
lemon juice

Place the milk, water, Cheddar, eggs and agar agar in a Thermomix and blend at 90°C on high speed for 10 minutes.

Remove and allow to cool: the mixture should resemble over-cooked scrambled eggs, and it will go quite stiff as it cools.

Re-blend in the Thermomix on high speed, adding salt and lemon juice to taste. Add a small amount of warm water if the custard is too thick or doesn't look smooth – it should look similar to a thick mayonnaise.

Maple Glaze

Makes about 100g

125g maple syrup
15g sherry vinegar

Heat the maple syrup and sherry vinegar together in a small pot on a medium heat and reduce until it has a syrupy consistency.

Beetroot, Smoked Yogurt, Lanark Blue

This is a Noto favourite, super easy to prep, and a bit of a crowd pleaser. I love beetroot in all forms – pickled beets from a jar are a go-to snack – and I could easily eat all four servings of this myself. Lanark Blue is made by the Errington Farm people, who make a handful of truly excellent cheeses in South Lanarkshire.

Serves 4 as a starter

½ recipe Roasted Red Beetroot (recipe follows)
½ recipe Light Pickled Golden Beetroot (recipe follows)
½ recipe Basic Vinaigrette (page 235)
1 recipe Smoked Yogurt (recipe follows)
Pickled Shallot Rings (page 222)
50g Lanark Blue
1 recipe Linseed Cracker (recipe follows)

1 candy cane beetroot

geranium flowers
watercress

Dress the red and golden beetroot in some of the vinaigrette and arrange on the plate. Top with smoked yoghurt and dress with pickled shallot rings. Crumble over small amounts of Lanark Blue and add layers of linseed crackers.

Slice the candy cane beetroot to 1mm thick on a mandolin and cut with a ring cutter. Dress the beetroot in a little more vinaigrette and lay on top of the salad. Finish with geranium flowers and some dressed watercress.

Roasted Red Beetroot

Makes 500g

100g salt
500g red beetroot
100g olive oil
2 sprigs of thyme

Preheat the oven to 180°C.

Line a baking tray with tin foil and cover with a generous layer of salt. Place the beetroot on top and drizzle with oil and thyme, then cover the tray tightly in tin foil and bake until the beetroot are tender (around 60 to 90 minutes).

Peel the beetroot while they're still warm, then allow to cool and cut them to shape.

Recipes continue on page 161

Light Pickled Golden Beetroot

Makes 500g

500g golden beetroot
50g sugar
25g salt
100g white wine vinegar
2kg water

Place the beetroot in a large pot with the sugar, salt, white wine vinegar and water. Boil until the beetroot are tender, adding more water to the pot as necessary to keep them covered so they cook evenly.

Once they are tender, drain and peel while still warm, then allow to cool before slicing.

Smoked Yogurt

Makes 100g

100g Skyr yogurt

wood chips
smoker or smoker gun

Spread the yogurt on a tray. Light the smoker, or use a smoker gun to smoke the yoghurt for 20 minutes.

Lineseed Cracker

Serves 4

50g linseed
50g hot water

sea salt

In a bowl, combine the linseeds and water and let sit for 15 minutes. Mix together with salt to taste.

Spread the mix on dehydrator trays as thinly as possible and place in the dehydrator overnight on high. You can also do this in an oven set to 70°C, but the crackers might not be as crispy.

Break the crackers into 6cm pieces.

Squash, Pear, Goat's Curds, Kinako Dressing

I often find salads pretty boring when I'm eating out, but this one ticks all the boxes. Roasting and blowtorching the squash gives it a depth of flavour that is sometimes missing, and the kinako dressing brings an almost peanut-buttery element to the dish. Good quality pears are essential.

Serves 4

1 recipe Roast Squash (recipe follows)
1 recipe Kinako Dressing (page 235)
20g fresh goat's or ewe's cheese curds
1 ripe pear
½ lemon
20g toasted hazelnuts, crushed
50g watercress (or any leaves you like)
10g Basic Vinaigrette (page 235)
10g pumpkin seeds, toasted

Scatter the roast squash pieces around each plate and drizzle them with kinako dressing. Top with scattered pieces of the crumbled cheese curds.

Cut the pear into quarters. Slice the seeds off, then cut each quarter lengthwise into very thin slices and squeeze the lemon over them. Place the pear on top of the salad.

Evenly sprinkle over the crushed, toasted hazelnuts, then top with the watercress dressed with a little vinaigrette and the toasted pumpkin seeds.

Roast Squash

Makes 500g

½ butternut squash (the bulb end)

50g olive oil
5g smoked paprika
3g garam masala
salt

blowtorch

Preheat the oven to 180°C.

Peel the bulb end of your butternut squash and cut it in half. Remove the seeds and then cut it on the diagonal into slices 1cm thick.

Toss the squash in oil and season with smoked paprika, garam masala and salt. Roast on a baking tray lined with parchment paper until tender, 20 to 30 minutes.

Remove the roast squash from the parchment and blowtorch the pieces until they are nicely charred. Serve at room temperature.

Scallops, Pumpkin, Yuzu Kosho

Hand-dived scallops are a treat. We are lucky to get such good quality ones in Scotland and I applaud the people who dive for them in all conditions. There's a reason why they're expensive – a lot of effort goes into getting them out of the water. I love to prep scallops, a legacy of my time at Gordon Ramsay's where we used to sell tons.

The key thing when you're cooking scallops is to sear them 75% on one side so they're nice and golden, then quickly flip them over to finish and be fast getting them out of the pan. We don't use the roe in this recipe, but in the restaurant they're not wasted: we might dry them then grind them up with salt to use as seasoning, or freeze them with liquid nitrogen and make granules to crust shellfish.

Serves 4

6 scallops in the shell
50g vegetable oil
½ lemon
1 recipe Brown Butter Pumpkin (recipe follows)
1 recipe Onion Rings (recipe follows)
1 recipe Yuzu Kosho Beurre Blanc (recipe follows)
50g Channel Wrack (recipe follows)
Dill Oil (page 231)
salt

Remove the scallops from their shells and trim off and discard all the connective tissues and the roe. Gently wash the scallops in lightly salted water and allow to dry on a cloth in the fridge to remove excess moisture. Store on a fresh cloth in the fridge.

To sear the scallops, cut each one in half so you have two flattish discs and season with some salt. Put a non-stick pan over a high heat and heat the vegetable oil until it's just about smoking. Put in the scallops and let them sear for 2 to 3 minutes. Once golden, flip them over for 30 seconds and then remove from the pan onto kitchen towel to drain. Squeeze a little lemon juice over the top.

Spoon some of the brown butter pumpkin into each bowl and arrange three scallop halves in a line over it. Top with onion rings, then gently drizzle the yuzu kosho beurre blanc sauce around the edge. Scatter over a little channel wrack and dot with dill oil.

Recipes continue on page 166

Brown Butter Pumpkin

Makes 500g

100g olive oil
500g pumpkin, cut into 1.2cm dice
salt

100g cold unsalted butter, diced

75g pumpkin seeds

juice of 1 lemon

5g dill, chopped
5g parsley, chopped
5g chives, chopped

Warm the oil in a sauté pan, then add the pumpkin and season with salt.

Cook gently over a medium heat, ensuring that you are moving the pan regularly so the pumpkin cooks evenly.

When the pumpkin starts to brown, add the butter and increase the temperature to medium–high to make the butter foam. Add the pumpkin seeds and continue to cook until the pumpkin is tender, stirring to ensure that the seeds get nicely toasted.

Add the lemon juice and remove from the heat. Allow to rest for 15 minutes, then add the chopped herbs.

Onion Rings

Makes 30g

30g shallots, cut into 2mm slices
300g milk

50g cornflour
50g potato starch
4g salt

sugar

vegetable oil for deep frying

Separate the shallot slices into rings and place in a bowl with the milk. Marinate for 30 minutes to take the harshness off the shallots.

Heat a deep fryer to 180°C. Mix the cornflour, potato starch and salt together in a bowl. Take the shallot rings from the milk and, whilst wet, dip them into the flour mix. Fry for 3 to 4 minutes until golden, then drain on kitchen towel and season with a little more salt and some caster sugar to taste.

Yuzu Kosho Beurre Blanc

Makes about 225g

50g Reduction (recipe follows)
75g double cream

150–200g cold unsalted butter, diced

yuzu kosho, approximately the size of an M&M

In a pan, heat the reduction and cream over a low heat and reduce by half, whisking regularly.

Whisk in the butter slowly, adjusting the consistency as necessary with a couple of drops of water. Season with yuzu koshu to taste.

Keep the beurre blanc warm until you need it. If it is allowed to cool completely it will split when re-heated.

Reduction

Makes 300–400g

50g vegetable oil
500g shallot, sliced
3g pink peppercorns
salt

1kg white wine

500g white wine vinegar

20g tarragon

In a medium-sized pot, heat the vegetable oil and sweat the shallots with the peppercorns and a little salt until they're soft but have no colour. Add the white wine and reduce by two thirds.

Add the vinegar and reduce by two thirds.

Remove from the heat and add the tarragon, then cover the pot with clingfilm and allow the reduction to steep for 15 minutes before straining.

Channel Wrack

Makes 50g

50g channel wrack, washed

vegetable oil to deep fry

Channel wrack is a very common seaweed that you see a lot on the rocks higher up the beach. We buy ours from local foragers who collect it from the coast near Edinburgh.

Dehydrate the channel wrack at 50°C for 6 to 8 hours or overnight.

Deep fry at 180°C for 10 seconds and drain on a tray lined with paper towels.

Buttermilk Fried Chicken, Tamarind, Coffee

Even though we had to take the fried chicken and waffles on page 41 off the menu at Noto, we kept the chicken element with the katsu sandwich on page 150 and this good and simple dish. Everyone has their preferred ways to serve fried chicken but this is my favourite. Use double the recipe of Buttermilk Fried Chicken.

Serves 4

2 × recipe Buttermilk Fried Chicken, made with 8 bone-in chicken thighs (page 41)
½ recipe Coffee Gastrique (recipe follows)

100g daikon
½ recipe Tamarind Mayo (page 234)
togarashi

spiraliser

Toss the hot fried chicken in a bowl with a couple of spoonfuls of the coffee gastrique. Roll the chicken around the bowl so all the pieces get some of the sticky glaze.

Peel the daikon and put it through a spiraliser to make into thin curly ribbons.

Place two pieces of chicken on each plate and top with a few dots of the mayo, a pile of daikon ribbons and a pinch of togarashi.

Coffee Gastrique

Makes about 200g

140g sugar
180g water

100g cabernet sauvignon vinegar

30g ground coffee

In a pot, boil the sugar and water until you have a dark caramel.

Deglaze with the vinegar, then infuse with the ground coffee for 5 minutes. Strain through a fine sieve.

Iberico Presa, Nahm Jim, Apple

Iberico presa is a fantastic cut of meat. It's cut from just below the tenderloin in the shoulder area and is sourced from acorn-fed pigs raised on sustainable farms, which gives it a rich and very nutty flavour. Keep it pink – around 62 to 65°C – and let it rest a decent amount of time to retain its juices. We source ours from Alternative Meats.

Serves 4

400g Iberico presa
salt
80g vegetable oil

60g unsalted butter, diced
2 sprigs of thyme

1 recipe Apple Gastrique (recipe follows)
1 recipe Nahm Jim (recipe follows)
100g radishes, shredded (any kind you like)
5g shiso
5g purple shiso
1 recipe Tamarind Compote (page 227)

Preheat the oven to 180°C.

Season the presa with salt. Heat a heavy frying pan and add the vegetable oil, then sear the meat until it is caramelised and golden all over. Add the butter and thyme to the pan and spoon it over the meat for 2 to 3 minutes, keeping the butter moving all the time so it doesn't burn.

Place the pork in the oven for 5 minutes, until it has an internal temperature of between 58 to 60°C. Rest for 6 to 7 minutes, then brush the meat with apple gastrique.

Slice the meat thinly into four slices. Top with half of the nahm jim dressing and layer some of the radishes on top, then add some more nahm jim and some shiso and purple shiso leaves. Place a spoonful of the tamarind compote on the side.

Recipes continue on page 172

Apple Gastrique

Makes approx. 250g

500g apple juice
50g brown sugar

100g chardonnay vinegar
salt

In pot, reduce the apple juice with the sugar until it reaches a tacky consistency. Deglaze with vinegar and season.

Nahm Jim

Makes about 100g

2 jalapeño chillies, deseeded and chopped
1 garlic clove, chopped
25g palm sugar

15g fish sauce
50g coriander, washed (leaves and stems)

25g lime juice

Blend the chilli, garlic and palm sugar together in a small food processor to make a paste. Add the fish sauce and coriander and pulse to incorporate. Add the lime juice and pulse to form a fine watery sauce. Season as necessary.

Chocolate, Miso, Hazelnut

When I was a kid, homemade chocolate mousse was a rare treat, but I also loved the very light Aero mousse pots we would get on the once-a-month big shop. I've always felt the judgement of any decent restaurant falls on its ability to make a decent chocolate mousse. This is a really good one: so simple, but absolutely delicious – using the best quality chocolate you can afford makes all the difference.

Serves 6

1 recipe Chocolate Mousse (recipe follows)
1 recipe Miso Caramel (recipe follows)
1 recipe Toasted Hazelnuts (recipe follows)
1 recipe Swiss Meringue (recipe follows)

blowtorch

Pipe spheres – approximately the size of an apple – of the chocolate mousse into each bowl. Dress the mousse with miso caramel, then scatter over enough toasted hazelnuts to cover. Pipe a swirl of Swiss meringue on top to resemble a snail's shell. Lightly blowtorch the meringue until golden brown.

Chocolate Mousse

Makes 500g

113g dark chocolate (72%)

150g double cream

3 egg whites
113g caster sugar

36g egg yolk

piping bag

Break up the chocolate and place into a bowl over a pot of gently simmering water, making sure the bottom of the bowl doesn't touch the water. Leave to melt.

In another bowl, gently whip the double cream to soft peaks, then put it in the fridge.

Start to whip up the egg whites (ideally with an electric whisk). Slowly add the sugar and keep whipping until you have soft peaks.

Beat the egg yolks in a large bowl, then mix in the melted chocolate. Fold in the whipped egg whites and, once incorporated, fold in the cold, softly whipped double cream.

Transfer the mousse into a piping bag (or leave it to set in six bowls or cups). Chill in the fridge until you are ready to serve.

Recipes continue on page 175

Miso Caramel

Makes 150g

120g sugar
50g water

40g white miso
95g sherry

In a medium pot, make a caramel with the sugar and water and cook until golden brown. Remove the pot from the heat and carefully add the miso and 70g of the sherry. Return to the heat to allow any sugar crystals to melt and bring the caramel to a thin syrup consistency. Add the remaining sherry and pass through a chinois before cooling.

Toasted Hazelnuts

Makes 200g

200g whole blanched hazelnuts

salt

Preheat the oven to 180°C. Toast the hazelnuts on a baking tray for 8 minutes, then shake to ensure even colouring and return to the oven for another 4 to 6 minutes until they are golden brown. Season while warm, then leave to cool and roughly chop.

Swiss Meringue

Makes 225g

75g sugar
75g liquid glucose
75g pasteurised egg white

piping bag

Over a double boiler, whisk the sugar, glucose and egg whites (preferably with an electric whisk) until all the sugar is dissolved and the meringue reaches a temperature of 50°C. Transfer to a stand mixer and whisk until cool, then transfer the meringue to a piping bag and store in the fridge until needed – it will last 24 hours.

Casual

Cooking staff tea is a really important skill in a restaurant kitchen, and just because chefs can cook amazingly high-end technical food, weirdly it doesn't mean they can make a decent staff tea. But for me, if a restaurant doesn't care about the staff eating well, it's not worth working at. It's generally the only thing we eat in the day, so it needs to be good, and it's when we all sit together, eat, unwind and have some family chat. A lot of kitchens see it as a hassle but literally the whole point of a restaurant is eating good food, and if staff tea is rubbish it kind of ruins the day.

This chapter is all about the dishes I cook in the restaurant for staff tea or at home for my wife and kids – things I like to eat or grew up eating. There's no pretension, no high-wire act, just solid recipes that appeal to all tastes and budgets.

Edinburgh
2023

Over time, I got better at being a chef and restaurant owner. I made all the mistakes and was lucky to have certain staff join me: Jade, Matt, Mark, Ash and Lewis were and are all heroes who have carried us to where we are now.

I'm not saying I'm not lucky, but I feel like being a bit naïve has actually helped me achieve things that I otherwise wouldn't have attempted. I think you can overthink things, see the potential obstacles and talk yourself out of trying. I always knew I could make the restaurants work: at every obstacle I just pretended that I knew it would be fine. You have to be a little tunnel visioned.

I know that reading a book like this can make things appear very linear and straightforward, but running restaurants is never like that. There's always a new issue with staffing, or suppliers, or the toilets, or some drunk or aggressive customer who needs to be thrown out, or someone who's chucked a lit cigarette down a drainpipe and it's made the inner walls catch fire and the fire brigade has to come out and I have to go in on my day off and then we get audited by the fire department (yes, this really did happen). It just never ends. As a chef–owner, I have to be a commis, a kitchen porter, a head chef, the HR department, a therapist, a plumber and a bouncer, sometimes all in the space of 30 minutes. But hey, that's why I love it.

I always planned to retire from the kitchen by the time I was 45, but my wife never believed I'd do it and it looks like she'll probably be right. I can't help eyeing up new sites and coming up with ideas for my next dream restaurant. It's easy to get caught up in this job but I try to remember, as a wise friend once told me, it's only cooking someone's tea.

Ajo Blanco

This chilled soup is a bit of magic, simultaneously light, bright and refreshing while still feeling substantial and satisfying. Originally hailing from Spain, ajo blanco belongs to warm summer evenings spent with good company. I like to garnish the soup with the same ingredients it's made from, to give texture and a fresh bite.

Serves 6

2 cucumbers, peeled, deseeded and chopped (approximately 350g prepped)
6 garlic cloves, chopped
125g crustless, day-old sourdough bread, cut into cubes
270g seedless green grapes, halved
180g blanched flaked almonds
345g extra virgin olive oil
35g sherry vinegar
5g salt
2g white pepper

750g whole milk

2 garlic cloves, finely sliced
4 green grapes, finely sliced
12 picked celery leaves
10g olive oil
10g almonds, roughly chopped
5g micro coriander or micro celery

In a large container, mix together the cucumber, garlic, sourdough, grapes, flaked almonds, olive oil, sherry vinegar, salt and white pepper. Cover and marinate for 3 hours at room temperature.

Put the mixture into a blender and pulse until smooth, then gradually add the milk until you have a soupy consistency. Pass it through a sieve to remove any lumps. If you're making this ahead of time, store it in the fridge and give it a little whisk before serving. You can also freeze it; just give it another blend when it has defrosted.

Pour the ajo blanco into bowls and top with slices of garlic and grapes, celery leaves, olive oil, chopped almonds and the micro greens.

Tomato Salad

Tomatoes are tricky: most are tasteless, full of water and not very ripe. So when Isle of Wight tomatoes are ready to go from the Tomato Stall people, it's an easy buy: they are readily available from around March-time. I really like to eat them with cheese curds, which have a good, creamy yet acidic flavour. You can usually buy curds from your local cheesemonger but, if you're struggling to find them, a crumbly-style goat's cheese would work. This is a simple but restaurant-worthy dish that's easy to make at home.

Serves 2

300g Isle of Wight tomatoes

½ recipe White Balsamic Vinaigrette (page 235)

50g goat's cheese curds
1 recipe Yellow Tomato Compote (recipe follows)
basil leaves
salad leaves, edible flowers or wild herbs

Skin the tomatoes by piercing the top and bottom with a sharp knife, then dropping them carefully into boiling water for 30 seconds. Drain, then pull off the skin. Place the skinned tomatoes in some iced water to cool, then halve or quarter depending on their size. Marinate the tomatoes in about 75g vinaigrette and leave to season for an hour.

Arrange the marinated tomatoes on a plate and spoon over more vinaigrette. Rip the cheese curds into bite-sized pieces and place around the tomatoes, then dot with spoonfuls of yellow tomato compote. Finish with basil and whatever salad leaves, edible flowers or wild herbs you have to hand.

Yellow Tomato Compote

Makes 200g

5 large yellow tomatoes

20g Scottish honey
27g olive oil
4 juniper berries
15g apple cider vinegar
salt

Peel the tomatoes as above and roughly chop. Put them in a small pot with the honey, olive oil, juniper and vinegar. Slowly simmer on a medium–low heat until the tomatoes break down and resemble a chutney. Blend in a small spice blender until smooth. Check the seasoning and adjust with salt and potentially a drop more vinegar.

Pâté en Croûte

I love a Gala pie. It's supermarket deli-counter genius food, and as kids we used to eat it all the time as part of a ploughman's-type dinner. Growing up in the kitchen I eventually realised that while pâté en croûte sounds fancy it is basically the same thing. It takes a bit of skill to make but ultimately is worth the hassle, so set aside a bit of time and enjoy the process.

Makes one medium-sized terrine (about 10 slices)

1 recipe Pastry (recipe follows)

1 recipe Pork Filling (recipe follows)
1 egg yolk
15g double cream

750g chicken stock, reduced by half (or 375g ready-made reduced stock)
4 leaves gold leaf gelatine

5–10g cabernet sauvignon vinegar

30cm terrine mould (or a 1kg loaf tin)

Preheat the oven to 210°C.

Roll out the pastry to roughly 2mm thick and cut off a piece the right size for the pie lid. Take the remaining pastry and lay it on top of your terrine mould or loaf tin, then press it in so it is flush with the bottom and sides.

Fill the lined terrine with the pork filling until it is completely full – you need to slightly overfill it as the filling will shrink during cooking.

Top the pie with the reserved piece of pastry and seal the edges, cutting off any excess. Beat the egg yolk and cream together, then brush the mix over the pastry lid. Make two 1cm holes in the lid to release any steam and to make it easier to pour in the jelly after cooking. An effective way of doing this is to wrap the end of a pen in tin foil, then push it through the pastry and into the filling, about a third of the way into the pie. Carefully pull the pen out, leaving the tin foil in the pie.

Bake for 15 minutes, then reduce the heat to 150°C for 20 minutes, then 90°C for another 30 minutes (or until a probe shows an internal temperature of 72°C). Leave to cool in the mould.

Once the pie is completely cold, prepare the jellied stock. In a pot, warm the reduced chicken stock. Soak the gelatine leaves in cold water to bloom for 5 minutes or until soft, then squeeze out the excess water and add them to the chicken stock. Stir until the gelatine has completely dissolved, then take the stock off the heat and season with a little vinegar just to balance the saltiness. Put it into a jug and leave to cool. Remove the tin foil from the holes in the pie lid. Once the stock is cool but before it has set, carefully and slowly pour it into the holes to fill any gaps between the pastry and the filling. You might not need all of the stock. Leave to set overnight before turning out the pie.

Pastry

Makes about 700g

375g plain flour
188g unsalted butter, cubed

86g whole milk
11g sugar
11g salt
1 egg
1 egg yolk

In a stand mixer with the paddle attachment fitted, mix the flour and butter until it resembles small breadcrumbs. Add the milk, sugar, salt, egg and egg yolk and mix until it comes together in a smooth paste. Wrap in clingfilm and rest in the fridge for 30 minutes.

Pork Filling

Makes about 1.5kg

20g brandy
20g port

700g pork shoulder, minced
325g pork belly, minced
300g pork belly, diced small
150g pancetta lardons
50g pork fat
60g shelled unsalted pistachios
10g sage, chopped
6g thyme, chopped
5g onion powder
3g mace powder
3g ground white pepper
2g Prague Powder #2 (optional)
2g salt (or 5g if you're not using Prague Powder #2)

You don't have to use the Prague Powder #2; however it really helps it to retain the pink colour in the meat and it also acts as a preservative. It's worth getting some as it's inexpensive, lasts forever and is really easy to find online.

In a very small pan, bring the brandy and port to the boil and reduce by half. Leave to cool.

Put all the remaining ingredients into a stand mixer and mix thoroughly, then mix in the reduced brandy and port.

Prosciutto and Tomato Herb Tart

Think of this as a tarted up quiche. Growing up, you could tell the days when things were a little tight financially because Mum would make a quiche – which was actually amazing because I loved it and it always generated lunch for the next day. This is a really simple tart and very cost-effective – with a little imagination it plates up to make an amazing restaurant-worthy lunch.

Serves 8

5 eggs, beaten
110g milk
220g double cream
250g Cheddar, grated
20g chives, finely chopped
10g parsley, finely chopped

1 recipe Parmesan Pastry Shell (recipe follows)

100g prosciutto
1 recipe Roast Cherry Tomatoes (recipe follows)
20g fresh herbs: (I use basil, chives, chervil, perilla, coriander)

Preheat the oven to 165°C.

In a large bowl, beat together the eggs, milk, cream, cheese, chives and parsley with a whisk until smooth. Put the Parmesan pastry shell, still in its tin, on a baking tray. Take the tray to the oven and place it on a shelf you have pulled out a little, then pour the egg mix into the pastry shell so it is as full as possible. Push the quiche fully into the oven and cook for 35 minutes until it is set – it should just wobble when you give it a shake.

Leave to cool at room temperature for 2 to 3 hours before cutting.

Cut the tart into eight slices and top each slice with some prosciutto: keep it wavy to give it some height. Top with four or five roast cherry tomatoes and then scatter over the herb salad.

Parmesan Pastry Shell

Makes 1 × 20cm tart shell

180g plain flour
100g cold unsalted butter, diced

50g Parmesan, grated
2 egg yolks
3g salt
20g chilled water

10g egg yolk
10g water

20cm tart tin (or springform cake tin)

Place the flour and butter into a stand mixer with the paddle attachment. Slowly mix until you have fine breadcrumbs. Add the Parmesan, egg yolks, salt and water and continue to mix until the dough forms a ball. Don't overwork the dough or it will crack, and be careful not to add the Parmesan, yolks, etc, until you have that fine breadcrumb texture. Wrap the dough in clingfilm and place in the fridge to relax for at least 30 minutes.

Rub a little butter into the tart tin, then dust it with a little flour and tip out the excess. Generously dust your work surface with flour and roll out the dough into a 45cm circle about 3mm thick. As you roll, keep turning and flipping the dough and re-flouring the surface to prevent sticking. Carefully lift the dough over the prepared tin and press it in so it is flush against the sides and base. Trim off any excess hanging over the edges of the tin and place in the fridge to chill for an hour.

Preheat the oven to 160°C. Once the tart shell is fully chilled, pierce the base and sides with a fork. Line the inside with a large piece of baking parchment, then fill with blind baking beans. Bake for 20 to 30 minutes until the outer edge of the crust begins to turn golden and the base no longer looks raw.

Once cooked, take the pastry shell out of the oven and leave it to cool for 10 to 15 minutes with the baking beans in place to keep the pastry flat. In a small bowl, mix together the 10g egg yolk and water. Once the pastry shell is cool, remove the parchment and beans and brush the inside of the shell evenly with the egg mix. Put it back in the oven for 2 to 3 minutes – this will create a waterproof seal to stop your tart filling from leaking out. Leave to cool in the tin.

Roast Cherry Tomatoes

Makes 150g

150g cherry tomatoes, split in half
6g caster sugar
6g salt
5g thyme leaves

Preheat the oven to 140°C. Line a baking tray with greaseproof paper.

In a bowl, mix the tomatoes with the sugar, salt and thyme. Lay in an even layer on the tray and roast for 15 minutes in the oven.

Kimchi

I love kimchi so much, and my wife Krystal often makes it at home. I was introduced to it by a friend called Walker in NYC. He was a great chef and used to show me all the NYC food spots, including a place called Hagi on West 49th between 6th and 7th Avenues which was open late nights, serving pitchers of Asahi beer, daikon salads, takoyaki balls and sides of kimchi. When I realised how easy it was to make and started learning the science around fermentation, I was hooked.

Makes 1 large jar

750g Chinese leaf cabbage
110g salt

6g ginger, grated
5 garlic cloves, microplaned
45g gochugaru dried Korean chilli flakes
8g golden caster sugar
5g dashi powder

300g daikon, peeled and cut into fine matchsticks
100g carrot, peeled and cut into fine matchsticks
4 spring onions, cut into 2.5cm pieces

1 × large (1.7–2L) Kilner jar

Cut the cabbage lengthways into quarters and remove the core. Cut each quarter across into 1cm-wide strips, then place into a large bowl with the salt. Massage the salt into the cabbage until it starts to soften a bit, then add enough water to cover. Cover with clingfilm, then put a plate on top and weigh it down with a heavy book or pan lid to keep the cabbage submerged. Leave to stand for 2 hours.

Rinse the cabbage with cold water three times, then allow to drain in a colander for 20 minutes.

Clean and dry the bowl, then add the ginger, garlic, gochugaru chilli flakes, sugar and dashi powder and mix into a paste. Add the drained cabbage and the daikon, carrot and spring onion.

Gently but thoroughly, work the paste into the vegetables until they are all well coated, then pack the kimchi tightly into your Kilner jar. Press it down in the jar until enough liquid rises to cover the vegetables, leaving at least 3cm space at the top of the jar – if not enough liquid is released, add a little water. Seal, and let the kimchi stand at room temperature for about 5 days. As it ferments, you should start to see some bubbles at the top. This is what you want.

Check the kimchi on day 3. It's good to open the jar a little to 'burp' it and release some of the gas that has been produced. Push down the vegetables again with a spoon to make sure they are still covered by liquid. After 5 days the kimchi will be ready – by now it should have a really nice sour taste. Store in the sealed Kilner jar in the fridge.

Bibimbap with Bacon and Eggs

This is a recipe to feed the troops – one of my go-tos for staff tea – packed with bright flavours and colourful vegetables, and topped with tender pork belly and an always-welcome fried egg. You can easily adjust the spice level to your preference and change out the vegetables as seasonally appropriate: the Korean word *bibimbap* means 'mixed rice' so there is no wrong way to enjoy it.

Serves 6

200g white sushi rice

1 recipe Pork Belly with Bulgogi Sauce (recipe follows)

30g vegetable/sunflower oil
6 eggs
salt
black pepper

1 recipe Carrot Salad (recipe follows)
1 recipe Pak Choi (recipe follows)
1 recipe Shiitake and Beansprout Salad (recipe follows)

1 recipe Gochujang Sauce (recipe follows)
4 spring onions, thinly sliced
10g coriander leaves

150g Kimchi (page 192)

Preheat the oven to 180°C.

Cook the rice according to the packet instructions and then keep it warm.

Heat a large non-stick frying pan over medium–high heat. Place strips of the pork belly in the pan and brown on both sides, 2 to 3 minutes each side. Transfer to a roasting pan and cover with the bulgogi sauce, then bake in the oven for 6 minutes. Turn the strips over and return to the oven for another 4 minutes.

Meanwhile, clean the frying pan and put it over a medium heat. Heat the oil and fry the eggs sunny side up, and season with salt and pepper.

Divide the steamed rice between six bowls. Arrange the carrot salad, pak choi and shiitake and beansprout salad in each bowl so that the rice is completely covered.

Brush the baked pork belly with gochujang sauce and cut each piece into three. Add four pieces to each bowl, then place a fried egg on top and garnish with spring onions and coriander leaves.

Serve with kimchi and the remaining gochujang sauce on the side.

Recipes continue on page 196

Pork Belly with Bulgogi Sauce

Serves 6

200g light soy sauce
180g brown sugar
200g apple juice

5 garlic cloves, crushed
10g fresh ginger, finely grated
15g sesame oil
3 spring onions, finely chopped

1kg boneless, skinless pork belly

25 × 25cm roasting tin

Mix together the soy, brown sugar and apple juice in a small saucepan and warm over a low heat until the sugar melts. Allow to cool and stir in the crushed garlic, ginger, sesame oil and spring onions. Pour this over the pork belly and leave to marinate in the fridge for 4 hours.

Preheat the oven to 150°C fan. Place the pork belly and marinade in the roasting tin, adding enough water to cover the meat completely. Cover tightly with tin foil and put in the oven to braise for 4 to 5 hours, checking regularly to see if you need to add more water.

Once the belly can be pierced with a small knife without any resistance, remove it from the oven and allow to rest for 30 minutes. Gently lift it out of the braising liquid onto a baking tray lined with baking parchment. Cover with another piece of parchment and put a baking tray on top, then add a weight – a pile of dinner plates would do – and leave until cool.

Strain the braising liquid through a fine chinois into a pan, then put it over a medium–high heat and reduce by two thirds to reach a thin sauce consistency. This is the bulgogi sauce.

Once the pork belly is cooled, portion into six slabs approximately 2cm thick.

Carrot Salad

Serves 6

2 large carrots, peeled

30g rice wine vinegar
10g honey
40g ginger, finely grated
2.5g salt

Grate the carrots on the large holes of a box grater. Dress with the rice vinegar, honey, ginger and salt and refrigerate until needed.

Pak Choi

Serves 6

500g pak choi, roughly chopped into 2cm pieces

25g light soy sauce
50g rice vinegar
25g toasted sesame oil
30g minced spring onions
30g sesame seeds, toasted
20g minced garlic

Blanch the pak choi in boiling salted water for 15 seconds. Cool in an ice bath, then drain and firmly squeeze to remove all excess water.

Put the pak choi in a bowl with the soy sauce, rice vinegar, sesame oil, spring onions, sesame seeds and garlic and leave to marinate for 15 minutes.

Shiitake and Beansprout Salad

Serves 6

100g sesame oil
40g light soy sauce
10g miso

10g sesame oil
100g shiitake mushrooms, cut into 1cm slices

300g beansprouts

4 shallots, finely diced
100g sesame seeds

Whisk the sesame oil with the soy sauce and miso until the miso has dissolved.

Heat a frying pan over a medium heat, then add the remaining 10g sesame oil and the shiitake mushrooms and fry for 2 to 3 minutes until the mushrooms are just soft. Set aside to cool.

Blanch the beansprouts in boiling salted water for 15 seconds and cool in an ice bath, then drain.

In a bowl, mix the mushrooms, beansprouts, shallots and sesame seeds together, then dress with the miso dressing.

XO Fried Rice

This is a real comfort dish, probably inspired by tons of takeaways over the years. Making the simple XO sauce gives it a nice edge.

Serves 4

80g sesame oil
3 eggs, beaten

60g vegetable oil
600g cooked white rice, cooled
1 recipe Quick XO Sauce (recipe follows)
150g frozen peas (defrosted)
3 spring onions, chopped

100g store-bought kimchi
30g coriander, chopped
1 lime, cut into quarters
1 red chilli, thinly sliced
2 spring onions, thinly sliced at an angle

Put a large frying pan over a high heat and add the sesame oil. Once hot, add the beaten eggs and scramble until they are set, then put them in a bowl and wipe out the pan.

Put the pan back over a high heat. Add the vegetable oil and, once hot, tip in the rice. As it starts to pop and heat up, stir in the XO, and then toss in the scrambled eggs. Once they are incorporated, add the peas and spring onions and keep stirring until everything is hot. Check the seasoning.

Pour the rice into bowls and top with a spoonful of kimchi, a sprinkle of chopped coriander, a lime wedge and some slices of red chilli and spring onion. Sometimes I leave out the scrambled eggs and top each bowl with a fried egg.

Quick XO Sauce

Serves 4

300g fresh prawns, peeled

45g sesame oil
1 onion, finely diced
3 carrots, peeled and finely chopped

4 garlic cloves, minced
100g best quality ham, diced

30g fish sauce
15g soy sauce
10g sugar
2g white pepper
2 green chillies, thinly sliced

Devein the prawns, then chop them into 1cm pieces.

Heat a large wok or frying pan until hot on a high heat and add the oil. Add the onion and carrot and fry, stirring until they start to colour, then add the garlic and ham and stir-fry for a minute more. Add the prawns and stir-fry for 1 minute or until they turn pink, then add the fish sauce, soy, sugar, pepper and chillies.

Boudin Blanc

During the course of my career, handmade sausages have been in steady decline as improved manufacturing processes have allowed restaurants to simply send their recipe to a butcher and *voilà* – perfection! Making sausages by hand is a messy, time-consuming process but you can't beat the satisfaction of turning all that mess into plump little bangers. I fully support a sausage revival.

Boudin blanc is the French sister to white pudding, with a substantial fat content. Bound with milk and cream, it is a good choice for a first foray into the sausage-making world. It doesn't require a press as the mixture does not need to be as densely packed into its casing as the traditional forcemeat counterpart. Although your local butcher may not have to hand all the things necessary to make the sausage, with a few days' notice they should be able to source everything for you (even the twine if you ask nicely).

Serves 4

4 Boudin Blanc (recipe follows)
30g vegetable oil
1 recipe Potato Mousseline (recipe follows)
1 recipe Prune Gravy (recipe follows)

Preheat the oven to 160°C.

Pan-fry the boudin blanc in vegetable oil until golden brown on all sides, then pop into the oven for 3 to 4 minutes to heat through. If need be, add a splash of milk to the potato mousseline to make it buttery and loose again, then put a generous spoonful of the mash on each plate. Top with a boudin blanc and pour over plenty of the prune gravy.

Recipes continue on page 202

Boudin Blanc

Makes 8 sausages

300g milk
1 onion, sliced
peel of 1 orange
3 bay leaves
3 sprigs thyme

½ onion, finely diced
20g butter
pinch of salt
pinch of sugar

400g pork leg, shoulder or loin, ground
150 pork fatback, ground
20g potato starch or breadcrumbs
20g salt
3g white pepper
pinch of nutmeg
180g egg whites
80g double cream

1 recipe Cooking Liquid (recipe follows)

2 × 1m sausage casings
piping bag with 1A hole tip
10 × 10cm lengths of butcher's twine

In a pan, warm the milk with the (sliced onion, orange peel, bay leaves and thyme) over a medium heat. Once it comes to a simmer, remove from the heat and allow to cool before straining. Discard the aromatics and keep the warmed milk to one side.

In another saucepan, sweat the diced onion with the butter over low heat. Add a pinch of salt and sugar and cook until soft and transparent but don't let anything brown. Remove from the pan and leave to cool.

Before you mix the sausage filling, prepare the casings by running cold water over them, then find the opening and place it directly under the running tap to force water through the entire length of the casing. Spray the opening with vegetable oil spray and run the oil through the length of the casing to help lubricate the stuffing process.

Mix the ground pork and fatback with the cooled onions, potato starch or breadcrumbs, salt, white pepper and nutmeg. Put the meat mixture into a blender and blend well. While the motor is running, add the egg whites and the warmed aromatic milk, and then the cream. Blend until just combined and store over ice until needed.

Fit a piping bag with a large round hole tip (1A size). Fill the bag with half the meat mix, then feed one end of the sausage casing onto the piping tip, scrunching it all over as tightly as possible. Trim any excess casing but don't tie off the end.

With your dominant hand holding the piping bag, gently squeeze, applying an even amount of pressure while slowly allowing the casing to unfurl as it fills. Make sure not to overfill the casings; the sausage at this point should feel a bit limp.

Once you have used all the mixture in the piping bag, tie off the casing at both ends. Divide into four linked sausages by tying with pieces of twine at roughly 10cm increments. Try to remove any visible air bubbles by poking a few holes along the length of the sausage with a toothpick, then set aside and repeat the process with the remaining meat mix.

Bring the cooking liquid to a low simmer (68–70 °C). Poach the sausages in the cooking liquid for 20 minutes, then place them in an ice bath to cool.

Drain the sausages on a tray lined with kitchen paper. Pat off any excess water and cut the links apart, removing the butcher's twine. Store, wrapped in clingfilm, in the freezer for up to a month.

Cooking Liquid

Makes 2.5kg

500g milk
2kg water
30g orange flower water

Mix the milk, water and orange flower water together in a large pot.

Potato Mousseline

Serves 4

100g salt
160g Albert Bartlett Rooster potatoes

150g cold unsalted butter, diced

60g double cream
60g whole milk
salt to taste

Preheat the oven to 160°C.

Line a baking tray with foil and sprinkle with the salt, then place the potatoes on top and bake in the oven for about 30 to 40 minutes, until they're soft in the middle when pierced with a fork.

Let the potatoes cool a little for 5 minutes or so, then cut them in half lengthways and scoop out the flesh into a potato ricer. Mill the potato through the ricer with the cold butter, then place in a medium-sized pot on a low heat.

In a separate small pot, bring the milk and cream to scalding and then slowly mix it into the mashed potato to make a smooth and silky mousseline. Keep warm until you're ready to serve.

Prune Gravy

Serves 4

250g Roast Chicken Stock (page 52)

10g cold unsalted butter, diced
5g sherry vinegar

5 prunes d'Agen, pitted and diced
5g parsley, chopped

Place the stock in a small pan and reduce until it starts to thicken. Once it is close to coating the back of a spoon, take it off the heat and whisk in the cold butter, then season with sherry vinegar. Fold in the prunes and parsley just before serving.

Butter Chicken Curry

I lived in Barbados for a few years when I was the chef de cuisine at Sandy Lane and it was an unforgettable experience. One of the great things about working with such a diverse workforce was the mix of local and expat chefs. The local chefs made the most amazing Caribbean curries with roti skins, and we also had a dedicated Indian chef who advised on the menus for the themed evenings in the casual restaurant. This is my favourite curry inspired by those times: it's an amalgamation of things I picked up from friends and colleagues and it beats any takeaway version.

Serves 4

30g vegetable oil
25g ginger, microplaned
25g garlic, microplaned

5g bay leaves
5g green cardamom pods
3g ground cinnamon

400g tinned chopped tomatoes

10g chilli powder
10g ground fenugreek
75g sugar
250g cold unsalted butter, cubed

125g double cream

1 recipe Chicken Tikka (recipe follows)

1 recipe Foolproof Rice (recipe follows)
1 recipe Cucumber and Yoghurt Chutney (recipe follows)
20g red onion, finely chopped
10g ginger, cut into fine matchsticks
10g micro coriander

4 Flatbreads (page 239)

Heat the vegetable oil in a deep saucepan over a medium heat. Fry off the ginger and garlic for a couple of minutes but don't let them burn or get too much colour. Add the bay, cardamom and cinnamon and toast for 2 to 3 minutes – this will help get the most flavour out of the spices.

Blend the tomatoes until smooth, then add them to the pan. Cook for 30 minutes on a medium to low heat. Add the chilli powder, fenugreek, sugar and butter and cook out for a further 5 minutes, then finish with the cream.

Pull the chicken tikka off the skewers and stir into the sauce. Serve on rice topped with cucumber and yoghurt chutney, a little finely chopped red onion and some sticks of ginger and micro coriander, with a flatbread on the side.

Chicken Tikka

Serves 4

150g yogurt
70g ginger paste
80g garlic paste
60g lemon juice
25g salt
20g cumin seeds, roasted and ground
10g deggi mirch
10g chaat masala
5g garam masala
5g ground fenugreek

8 boneless, skinless chicken thighs

4 bamboo skewers, soaked in cold water overnight

A lot of the taste and colour here comes from two spices: deggi mirch and chaat masala. Deggi mirch is a bright red chilli powder that comes from red peppers and Kashmiri chilli. Chaat masala is a spice mix with black salt, dried mango powder, chilli, cumin and a few other spices. It has a really funky smell and a sour, salty but slightly sweet flavour and is often used in fruit preparations in South Asia. You should be able to find them in any Indian or Middle Eastern grocers.

In a large bowl, mix together the yoghurt, ginger, garlic, lemon juice, salt, cumin, deggi mirch, chaat masala, garam masala and fenugreek. Cut each chicken thigh into four pieces and add to the yoghurt mix. Rub it thoroughly into the chicken and leave to marinate for at least 3 to 4 hours and preferably overnight.

Turn your grill to the highest setting. Push the marinated chicken pieces onto skewers so they are packed tight and place on a baking tray lined with tin foil.

Grill the chicken for about 20 minutes until the meat has an internal temperature of 75°C, turning every so often to get an even browning. Ideally you want some charred bits (this is a good time to use a BBQ grill).

Foolproof Rice

Serves 4

1 measuring cup basmati rice
2 measuring cups water

Wash the basmati rice in a sieve, running water through it until it is clear. Add to a pot and cover with the measured 2 cups of water. Bring to a rapid boil and cover with a lid or a sheet of tin foil. Turn the heat down to the lowest you can go and let it cook for 10 minutes – you should stop seeing steam evaporating from the pan. Turn off the heat and leave the lid on for 5 minutes before fluffing with a fork and serving.

Cucumber and Yoghurt Chutney

Makes about 300g

200g cucumber

20g picked mint leaves
200g Greek yoghurt
5g ground cumin
10g lemon juice
10g garlic, grated
salt

Peel the cucumber and slice it in half lengthways. With a small spoon, scrape out the seeds, then chop the flesh into small dice. Put in a bowl.

Finely chop the mint and add to the bowl, then mix in the Greek yoghurt, cumin, lemon juice and garlic. Season with a little salt.

Custard Tart

It seems that every culture has independently discovered the beauty of sweet egg custard. A custard tart works on a restaurant menu as well as it does at home, and a version featured in my trial for Sandy Lane, plated with saffron compressed pineapple, ginger crémeux and brown butter ice cream.

The hardest part of this recipe is waiting for it to cool completely before cutting. Feel free to use a deep, pre-baked tart shell if you don't have the time or desire to make your own sweet paste.

Serves 6–8

1 egg
160g egg yolks (roughly 8–10 yolks)
75g caster sugar

500g double cream

1 Sweet Tart Shell (recipe follows)
1 whole nutmeg

20g caster sugar

blowtorch

Preheat the oven to 150°C.

In a large bowl, whisk together the whole egg, egg yolks and sugar. Place the double cream in a pot and heat to just before boiling point, then slowly pour it over the eggs while whisking. Strain through a fine chinois back into the pot and cook out on a low heat for 5 minutes.

Carefully, pour the mixture into the baked tart shell and grate nutmeg all over the top so the surface is entirely covered. Bake in the oven for 40 minutes, until the custard is set.

Allow the tart to cool completely on a wire rack before removing from the tin. Glaze the tart before you slice it: gently sprinkle the caster sugar over the custard and torch with a blowtorch until brûléed. The tart can be stored in the fridge in an airtight container for up to 3 days.

Sweet Tart Shell

Makes 1 tart shell

165g plain white flour
50g caster sugar
1g salt

83g cold unsalted butter, diced

1 egg

1 egg yolk
15g water

34 × 13cm tart tin (or 20cm springform cake tin), greased and lined

In a stand mixer with the paddle attachment, mix together the flour, sugar and salt. Add the butter and mix until it is completely incorporated – the mixture should look like damp sand. Add the egg and continue to mix until a dough begins to form. Wrap tightly in clingfilm and refrigerate for at least 1 hour.

Generously dust your work surface with flour and roll out the sweet paste dough until it is about 3mm thick. As you roll, keep turning and flipping the dough and re-flouring the surface to prevent sticking. Carefully lift the dough over the prepared tin and press it in so it is flush against the sides and base. Trim off any excess hanging over the edges of the tin and freeze for 30 minutes.

Preheat the oven to 170°C. Once the tart shell is fully chilled, pierce the base and sides with a fork and line the inside with a large piece of baking parchment, then fill with blind baking beans. Bake for 20 minutes until the outer edge of the crust begins to turn brown, then remove the beans and parchment. Return the tart shell to the oven and bake for another 15 to 20 minutes, until the base is light brown and completely cooked.

Mix the egg yolk and water and brush it lightly all over the inside of the tart shell to seal it. Return the shell to the oven for another 2 to 3 minutes.

You can either use the shell right away or prepare it in advance and allow to cool. It will keep in an airtight container at room temperature for up to 5 days.

Chocolate Tart

'If this book was a wardrobe, this chocolate tart would be your good coat. It goes with everything and is guaranteed to receive plenty of compliments.'

Ash Fahy, former Aizle and Noto legend

Serves 12

200g Oreo biscuits
50g unsalted butter, melted

320g 72% dark chocolate, roughly chopped
75g cold unsalted butter, diced
340g double cream
25g glucose

flaked sea salt
1 recipe Chantilly Cream (recipe follows)
5g best quality cocoa powder

20cm springform cake tin, greased and lined

Preheat the oven to 180°C.

In a food processor, blitz the Oreos to make a fine crumble, then mix in the melted butter and press into the base of the prepared tin using the back of a spoon. Bake for 8 minutes and allow to cool.

Place the dark chocolate and diced butter in a large bowl. In a medium pan, carefully heat the cream and glucose to a boil, then immediately pour it over the chocolate and stir until the chocolate and butter have melted and everything is well combined. Pour onto the Oreo base, gently tapping the tin against the work top to remove any air bubbles.

Leave for at least 6 hours to set completely. If it's still a little soft, put it in the fridge for 20 minutes, then leave out for 30 minutes to come back to room temperature.

Serve small slices scattered with a few flakes of sea salt, and a little Chantilly cream dusted with cocoa on the side.

Grown-up variation: reduce the amount of double cream to 300g and add 60g of your chosen alcohol into the cream mixture – Drambui, Cointreau and Kahlúa are all good choices.

Chantilly Cream

Makes 250g

250g whipping cream
1 vanilla pod
8g icing sugar

Put the cream in a large bowl. With a sharp knife, scrape out the seeds from the vanilla pod and add them to the bowl along with the icing sugar. Whip everything together, making sure the sugar is completely dissolved, until a heavy ribbon stage is achieved.

Doughnuts

There is no denying that doughnuts are happy food. They make me think of holidays in Cornwall when I was a kid, when my mum would always buy us a bag of saffron doughnuts from the bakery in Newlyn, not far from our family home, Old Kent House.

This recipe makes twenty doughnuts, which might seem excessive, but I have never had any leftovers. The dough itself is not overly sweet, allowing you to fill, glaze and decorate to your heart's content. My favourite way to eat them is warm from the fryer with a generous dusting of icing sugar – one perk to being the chef is I don't have to share if I don't want to. The cool doughnuts will keep in an airtight container for 3 days.

Serves 6–8

63g warm water
7g fresh yeast or 3.5g dry active yeast
125g flour

....

7g fresh yeast or 3.5g dry active yeast
60g milk, cold
250g flour
45g sugar
5g salt
54g egg yolk
30g butter, melted

....

vegetable oil for deep frying

....

1 recipe Spicy Sugar (recipe follows)
1 recipe Vanilla Cream (recipe follows)
1 recipe Blueberry Jam (recipe follows)

....

2 baking trays, lined with greaseproof paper

Mix together the warm water, yeast and 125g flour in a bowl, and then cover with clingfilm and prove for an hour.

In a stand mixer with dough hook attachment, add the second quantity of yeast, milk, 250g flour, sugar, salt, egg yolks and melted butter to the proved sponge and mix until it forms a smooth elastic dough. Cover with clingfilm and prove for another hour.

Lightly spray your work surface with oil and turn out the dough on top, then portion it into 30g pieces. Cup your hand over one of the pieces, pressing the heel of your hand against the table. Move your hand in small concentric circles while applying a light amount of pressure to make a springy round ball. Place on the lined baking tray and repeat to shape all the remaining pieces of dough. Gently cover with clingfilm and prove for an hour.

Preheat a deep fryer to 170°C and line two baking trays with kitchen paper. Gently drop a few dough balls into the fryer and cook for 2 to 3 minutes until golden brown, then flip and cook for another few minutes until evenly browned all over. Lift the doughnuts from the oil with a slotted spoon and put on the kitchen-paper-lined trays to drain. As you fry the rest of the doughnuts, make sure the oil stays at a consistent 170°C.

Roll the warm doughnuts in the spicy sugar and serve with vanilla cream and blueberry jam on the side for dipping them into. Don't be shy with the toppings! If you want to fill the doughnuts instead, make a hole in the side with a small knife and slowly pipe in the filling until they are nice and swollen.

Spicy Sugar

Makes 200g

200g caster sugar
7g cinnamon
7g allspice

Mix the sugar, cinnamon and allspice and store in an airtight jar.

Vanilla Cream

Serves 6–8

1 sheet gold leaf gelatine

60g egg yolk
15g caster sugar

200g double cream
1 vanilla pod, seeds scraped out with a sharp knife

Soak the gelatine in a bowl of cold water until it is soft.

In a bowl, whisk the egg yolks and sugar until smooth. Put the cream and vanilla seeds and pod in a pot and bring to a boil. Slowly pour the hot cream over the yolks and sugar, whisking well, and return the mix to the pot. On a low heat, bring the mixture to 82°C, whisking all the time.

Squeeze the gelatine to remove any excess water, then whisk it into the custard. Remove the vanilla pod and leave to cool. Once cold, gently whisk until you have a smooth cream. If you want to fill the doughnuts, place the cream in a piping bag.

Blueberry Jam

Serves 6–8

60g sugar
34g water
35g cider vinegar

185g blueberries
5g ground cinnamon
2g allspice
1g cloves

zest of ½ a lemon

In a medium-sized pot, add the sugar, water and vinegar and bring to a boil. Stir in the blueberries, cinnamon, allspice and cloves and cook out fast until the sauce reduces and thickens to a maple-syrup-like consistency. Add the lemon zest, then leave to cool. If you want to fill the doughnuts, place the jam in a piping bag.

Miso Chocolate Fudge

'Oh fudge!' has always felt a rather appropriate kid-safe expletive, as fudge has a lot in common with a toddler: it requires constant supervision and stimulation, and trying to rush it will likely end in a tantrum. Patience is required for this recipe, but you will be rewarded with a goodly amount of moreish morsels.

Makes 100 pieces

300g 72% dark chocolate, chopped

158g double cream
205g caster sugar
128g glucose syrup

90g unsalted butter, diced
45g yellow miso

flaked sea salt

20 × 20cm tin, lined with greaseproof paper

Put the chocolate in a bain marie to melt, and once fully melted keep it warm over a low heat.

In a medium pot, mix together the double cream, sugar and glucose and begin to cook over a medium heat, stirring all the time to prevent it burning. Probe the mix regularly with a thermometer; once it reaches 108°C, reduce the heat to low and continue to cook until it reaches 120°C.

Stir in the butter and bring the mixture back to 120°C over a low heat. Take off the heat and add the warm melted chocolate and the yellow miso, stirring until the miso has fully dissolved.

Pour the fudge into your prepared tin and sprinkle a few flakes of sea salt on top. Leave to cool for 4 hours before cutting into 2cm squares. Store in an airtight container for up to 2 weeks (some chance).

Pickles and Chutneys

Acidity is one of the biggest flavour profiles I focus on when I'm cooking. As a kid, I would always get pickled onions and pickled eggs from the chippy and now all my dishes have high acidity: Granny Smith apples, rhubarb, pickles and sauces finished with vinegars are all regulars on our menus. When I worked in NYC, chef Markus Glocker would always yell, 'Ways more acids, yah!' in his Austrian accent – he also felt passionate about the amount of acidity in food. Acidity can keep the richest of foods balanced and really bring things to life; a squeeze of lemon juice on some smoked salmon or a little mignonette on an oyster really helps to lift the flavours and create a more complex dynamic. Think of Branston pickle on a little cheese – these combos are everywhere and they work for a reason.

Pickle Liquor

Makes about 400g

200g water
160g white wine vinegar
45g sugar
15g salt
5g star anise
5g coriander seeds
5g juniper seeds
5g black peppercorns
3g green cardamom pods
2g pink peppercorns

Place the water, white wine vinegar, sugar, salt and spices in a pot and bring to a boil. Boil for 5 minutes, whisking to dissolve the sugar and salt, and then leave to cool.

Pickled Mustard Seeds

Makes 50g

200g Pickle Liquor (recipe above)
50g yellow mustard seeds

Place the pickle liquor and mustard seeds in a medium-sized pot and bring to a boil.

Turn down the heat to medium and simmer for 15 minutes, then take the pot off the heat and leave to cool. Store in an airtight jar.

Pickled Shallot Rings

Makes about 200g

400g Pickle Liquor (recipe above)
1 beetroot, thinly sliced

4 shallots, sliced into 2mm rings

In a small pot, bring the pickle liquor to a boil with the sliced beetroot so it is infused with red. Strain the liquor while it's hot, then pour it over the shallot rings. Cover with clingfilm and allow to cool. Store in an airtight jar for up to a month.

Pickled Shimeji Mushrooms

Makes 150g

150g shimeji mushrooms

200g Pickle Liquor (recipe above)

Prepare the mushrooms by cutting each one from the stem. Place into a bowl or jar.

Heat the pickle liquor and, once it reaches a boil, strain and pour over the mushrooms. Cover with clingfilm and allow to cool.

Once cool, store the mushrooms in an airtight container in the fridge for up to a month.

Pickled Silverskin Onions

Makes 250g

250g silverskin onions

400g Pickle Liquor (page 222)
1 beetroot, thinly sliced

Prepare the onions by peeling off the outer skin and then cutting them in half lengthways.

In a small pot, bring the pickle liquor to a boil with the sliced beetroot so it is infused with red. Strain the liquor while it's hot, then pour it over the prepared onions and cover with clingfilm. Allow to cool. Store in a jar in the fridge for up to a month.

Pickled Wild Leeks

Makes 200g

400g Pickle Liquor (page 222)

200g wild leeks, cleaned

Bring the pickle liquor to the boil. Place the leeks in a sterilised jar, then pour the hot pickling liquor over the top, making sure they're entirely covered. Seal and keep in the fridge or dry store for up to 3 months.

Compressed Cucumber

Makes about 175g

1 cucumber, peeled

45g Pickle Liquor (page 222)
15g Dill Oil (page 231)

Cut the cucumber in four lengthways and remove the seeds. Finely cut the flesh into 2mm dice. Cover with pickling liquor and dill oil and, if available, place in a chamber vacuum machine to compress. It is ready to eat straight away but you can store it in an airtight container for 2 days (though it might start to go brown or soft after this).

Compressed Cucumber and Kohlrabi

Makes 200g

100g cucumber
100g kohlrabi

45g Pickle Liquor (page 222)

Peel the cucumber, then cut in four lengthways and remove the seeds. Finely cut the flesh to 2mm dice.

Peel the kohlrabi and, using a Parisian scoop, scoop out little balls.

Cover both with pickle liquor and, if available, place in a chamber vacuum machine to compress. Store in an airtight container for 2 days.

Pickled Lettuce

Makes about 200g

2 organic Little Gem lettuce, cut into quarters lengthways
100g Pickle Liquor (page 222)

Vacuum pack the lettuce wedges with the cold pickle liquor.

PICKLE
SHIMEJI
7/12 - 8/12

Pickled Radicchio

Makes 100g

100g radicchio, separated into leaves
100g Pickle Liquor (page 222)

Vacuum pack the radicchio with the cold pickle liquor.

Pickled Red Chicory

Makes 100g

100g red chicory, cut into leaves
100g Pickle Liquor (page 222)

Vacuum pack the red chicory with the cold pickle liquor.

Pickled Sliced Beetroot

Makes 100g

100g peeled beetroot, sliced to 1mm on a Japanese mandolin
100g Pickle Liquor (page 222)

Vacuum pack the sliced beetroot with the cold pickle liquor.

Pickled Wild Leek Buds

Makes 50g

50g wild leek buds
200g salt

25g white wine vinegar
25g sugar
50g water

Wild leek buds are nature's candy! Wild garlic and leeks are only in season in Scotland for a few months from the middle/end of February, and towards the end of the season they develop the hard little caper buds that you need here. I salt them before putting them in a small amount of pickling liquid and they keep for months.

Bury the wild leek buds in a container of salt for 6 weeks, then rinse the salt off.

Combine the white wine vinegar, sugar and water in a small pot and bring to a boil to dissolve the sugar. Allow it to cool before pouring over the wild leek buds. In the restaurant we vacuum pack them, but you can also put them in a jar and they'll be ready to eat in a few days.

Black Garlic Condiment

Makes 250g

125g water
65g sugar
65g white wine vinegar
4g agar agar

25g black garlic, peeled

In a medium-sized pot, mix the water, sugar and vinegar. Whisk in the agar agar and bring to a boil, then pour into a container and allow it to go cool. It will set to quite a hard gel.

With a hand blender, blend the gel with the black garlic until smooth, then pass it through a sieve to remove any small lumps. Store in a jar in the fridge for 2 weeks.

Burnt Apple Ketchup

Makes about 300g

1kg Granny Smith apples
100g brown sugar

30g seedless tamarind pulp
100g water
80g vegetable oil

cider vinegar
salt

Preheat the oven to 180°C.

Roughly chop the unpeeled apples and toss with the brown sugar in a roasting tin. Bake in the oven for about 40 to 60 minutes until they are caramelised.

Scrape the cooked apples into a blender with the tamarind and blend until smooth, adding the water and oil as necessary to get the consistency you want. Once smooth, season with cider vinegar and salt. Store in a jar in the fridge for 2 weeks.

Umeboshi Purée

Makes about 200g

5 plums

60g vegetable oil
1 medium white onion, diced

3g ground cinnamon
3g ground ginger
3g ground allspice
3g ground coriander

75g umeboshi plums, rinsed and chopped small

L&P Worcestershire sauce
sherry vinegar
salt

Preheat the oven to 180°C. Place the five whole plums in a roasting tin and bake until they explode and their skin turns black, approximately 1 hour.

In a pot over a medium heat, heat the vegetable oil and then sweat the onion without colour until soft. Add the cinnamon, ginger, allspice and coriander and continue to cook for 5 minutes until it begins to catch, then stir in the chopped umeboshi plums and enough water to just cover. Cook on a low heat until the umeboshi are well incorporated. Add more water as necessary to prevent it from sticking to the bottom of the pan.

Discard the stones from the baked plums, then add the plums to the pot, scraping in any residue from the baking tray. Continue to cook on low heat until you have a thick paste, approximately 30 to 40 minutes.

While the mixture is warm, place it in a blender and purée on high for 5 minutes until smooth. Season with L&P sauce, sherry vinegar and salt, then pass the purée through a fine chinois. Store in an airtight container in the fridge for up to 2 weeks.

Cherry Mustard

Makes 500g

80g vegetable oil
4 shallots, finely diced
1 fennel, finely diced

2g ground allspice
2g black peppercorns
2g juniper berries
2g coriander seeds

100g cabernet sauvignon vinegar
80g pinot noir
1 recipe Brined Cherries (recipe follows)

70g cherry purée
80g grain mustard

This mustard is worth its weight in gold. It works particularly well with beef but is also delicious with cheese and some biscuits. I have used this recipe for years and it always makes an appearance at Aizle.

In a medium pot, heat the oil and then sweat down the shallot and fennel until they are translucent with no colour. Add the allspice, black peppercorns, juniper and coriander seeds and mix well to combine.

Deglaze with the vinegar and pinot noir and add the brined cherries (including their liquid). Continue to cook on low heat until very jammy, then stir in the cherry purée and grain mustard. Store in the fridge in a jar for up to 3 months.

Brined Cherries

250g dried sour cherries
135g cabernet sauvignon vinegar
75g cherry purée
65g water
65g sugar

In a large pot, bring the dried cherries, vinegar, cherry purée, water and sugar together to a boil. Remove from the heat, cover with clingfilm and leave to hydrate for 2 hours.

Tamarind Compote

Makes about 250g

230g seedless tamarind pulp
150g water

25g palm sugar
5g caster sugar
10g garam masala
salt to taste

Place the tamarind pulp in small pot and cover with the water. Boil for 20 minutes, then add the palm sugar, caster sugar, garam masala and salt and cook for 5 minutes until it has reached a thick chutney consistency. Transfer to a bowl and serve cold.

Oils and Emulsions

We make a lot of flavoured oils in the restaurants: they're a great way to preserve herbs and a few drops can really enhance a finished dish. The oils can be used on their own and in salad dressings, you could also finish soups with them or put a few drops on fresh pasta.

Thickened with egg yolk, the flavoured oils become emulsions: sauces with a mayonnaise-y texture that carry flavours really well. Just a small amount can give a luxurious feel to the most simple dish.

Dill Oil

Makes about 400g

100g picked dill
100g picked parsley

400g pomace oil

Blanch the dill and parsley in boiling salted water for 30 seconds, then cool in an ice bath. Squeeze out the herbs to remove all excess water and roughly chop.

Put the blanched herbs and oil in a Thermomix and blend at 80°C for 5 minutes on high. Immediately transfer to a strainer lined with a j-cloth. Allow the oil to drain through until only the herb residue remains in the j-cloth, approximately 1.5 hours.

This will keep for 5 days in the fridge or 1 month in the freezer.

Herb Oil

Makes about 400g

100g picked parsley
25g picked mint
25g picked lovage

400g pomace oil

Blanch the parsley, mint and lovage in boiling salted water for 30 seconds, then cool in ice water. Squeeze out the herbs to remove all excess water and roughly chop.

Put the blanched herbs and the pomace oil in a Thermomix and blend at 80°C for 5 minutes on high. Immediately transfer to a strainer lined with a j-cloth. Allow the oil to drain through until only the herb residue remains in the j-cloth, about 1.5 hours.

This will keep for 5 days in the fridge or 1 month in the freezer.

Lovage Oil

Makes about 400g

100g picked lovage
100g picked parsley

400g pomace oil

Blanch the lovage and parsley in boiling salted water for 30 seconds, then cool in an ice bath. Squeeze out the herbs to remove all excess water and roughly chop.

Put the herbs and oil in a Thermomix and blend at 80°C for 5 minutes on high. Immediately transfer to a strainer lined with a j-cloth. Allow the oil to drain through until only the herb residue remains, approximately 1.5 hours.

Store for 5 days in the fridge or 1 month in the freezer.

Dill Emulsion

Makes 275g

50g egg yolk
15g Dijon mustard
10g white wine vinegar
200g Dill Oil
salt

With a hand blender, blend the egg yolks, mustard and vinegar. Still blending, slowly add enough dill oil for it to form stiff peaks. Season to taste.

Egg Yolk Emulsion

Makes about 280g

200g pomace oil
6 egg yolks, unbroken

25g chardonnay vinegar
salt

At our restaurants we vacuum seal the egg yolks, then cook them in a water bath at 68°C for 90 minutes. A similar result can be achieved at home by making confit egg yolks.

Place the pomace oil in a small saucepan and carefully drop the egg yolks into the pot. Gently heat the oil to 65°C and cook for 55 minutes on a low heat. With a spoon, remove the yolks from the oil and allow both to cool.

With a hand blender, pulse the egg yolks until smooth and then, while blending, add the oil slowly to form a thick emulsion. Season with chardonnay vinegar and salt.

Herb Emulsion

Makes about 275g

50g egg yolk
15g Dijon mustard
15g chardonnay vinegar
200g Herb Oil (page 231)
salt

With a hand blender, blend the egg yolks, mustard and vinegar. Still blending, slowly add enough herb oil for it to form stiff peaks. Season to taste.

Lovage Emulsion

Makes 275g

50g egg yolk
15g Dijon mustard
10g white wine vinegar
200g Lovage Oil (page 231)
salt

With a hand blender, blend the egg yolks, mustard and vinegar. Still blending, slowly add enough lovage oil for it to form stiff peaks, season.

Mustard Emulsion

Makes 290g

50g egg yolks
15g Dijon mustard
15g wholegrain mustard
10g white wine vinegar
200g pomace oil
salt

With a hand blender, blend the egg yolks, Dijon and wholegrain mustards and vinegar. Still blending, add the oil until it forms stiff peaks, then season.

Beef Fat Mayo

Makes 275g

25g Rendered Beef Fat (recipe follows)
175g pomace oil

50g egg yolk
15g Dijon mustard
10g white wine vinegar

salt

Place the rendered fat and pomace oil in a pot and gently warm to melt the beef fat.

With a hand blender, blend the egg yolks with the mustard and vinegar, then slowly add enough of the beef fat mix for it to form stiff peaks. Season with salt as necessary.

Rendered Beef Fat

Makes more than you need but it will keep in the fridge for up to 3 months

200g beef fat, roughly diced

You can buy rendered beef fat at any good butchers, but it is easy to make yourself.

In a large pot, slowly melt the beef fat over a low heat. It will probably take up to about 1 hour to fully render. Pass the rendered fat through a strainer lined with muslin cloth to remove any remaining solids.

Kewpie Mayo

Makes about 325g

50g egg yolk
15g white wine vinegar
15g Dijon mustard
45g sugar
200g pomace oil
salt

Blend the egg yolks on low, then add the vinegar, mustard, sugar and a little salt.

While blending, slowly add the pomace oil until a thick mayonnaise forms, then adjust seasoning as necessary.

Onion Mayo

Makes 355g

50g egg yolks
15g white wine vinegar
sugar
salt

15g Dijon mustard
200g pomace oil
75g Onion Purée (recipe follows)

With a hand blender, blend the egg yolks, then mix in the vinegar, mustard and a pinch of sugar and salt. Still blending, slowly add enough pomace oil for a thick mayonnaise to form.

Add the onion purée and adjust seasoning as necessary. Place into piping bags until needed.

Onion Purée

Makes about 300g

100g vegetable oil
1kg large white onions, sliced
1 bay leaf
15g thyme
12g salt
5g black pepper

200g white wine

50g sherry vinegar

In a large pot over a medium heat, warm the oil and add the sliced onions, bay leaf and thyme. Lightly season with the salt and black pepper and allow to sweat, stirring regularly.

Continue sweating the onions until they begin to colour and stick to the bottom of the pot, about 20 minutes. Deglaze with the white wine and scrape down the base of the pot.

Continue to cook slowly, stirring often. If the onions begin to stick add 50g of water to the pot to stop them burning. Cook for 1 hour until the mixture is a dark brown colour.

Remove the bay leaf and thyme and discard. Blend the onions into a smooth purée - you may need to add a small amount of warm water to assist with the blending. Add sherry vinegar to taste and adjust seasoning as necessary.

Tamarind Mayo

Makes 275g

50g egg yolks
5g white wine vinegar
5g Dijon mustard
200g pomace oil
15g tamarind paste
salt

With a hand blender, blend the egg yolks with the vinegar and mustard. Still blending, slowly add the pomace oil until a thick mayonnaise forms, then add the tamarind paste and season to taste.

Miso Mustard Mayo

Makes 255g

30g white miso
15g Dijon mustard
25g egg yolk
10g rice wine vinegar
175g pomace oil

With a hand blender, blend the miso, mustard, egg yolk and vinegar. Still blending, add enough of the pomace oil for the mayo to form stiff peaks.

Place in a piping bag and store in the fridge for up to 3 days.

Basic Vinaigrette

Makes 450g

60g Dijon mustard
50g white wine vinegar
60g water
14g sugar
4g salt
270g vegetable oil

In a bowl, whisk together the mustard, vinegar, water, sugar and salt, then slowly whisk in the oil.

White Balsamic Vinaigrette

Makes 260g

100g white balsamic vinegar
100g olive oil
50g pomace oil
5g lemon juice
10g sugar

2 sprigs of basil
salt and pepper to taste

In a small bowl, whisk the vinegar, olive and pomace oils, lemon juice and sugar together. Crush the basil leaves with your hands and add to the dressing, then leave to infuse for 20 minutes. Remove the basil before using and season with salt and pepper.

Kinako Dressing

Makes about 120ml

10g kinako
2g ground ginger
50g pomace oil
25g sesame oil
35g rice wine vinegar
salt

Kinako is just roasted soy bean flour, a nutty powder that adds a ton of flavour to dishes.

Whisk the kinako, ground ginger, pomace and sesame oils and rice wine vinegar together, ensuring there are no lumps. Season as necessary. It should be a similar consistency to a pesto.

Breads

There's a lot of satisfaction to be had from making your own bread; for me it comes from knowing that with only a few key ingredients – good quality flour, salt, yeast and water – you can make something so delicious. Here are six recipes to suit different styles of dining, all using very practical and simple techniques to achieve good quality bread at home. Bread is something I would struggle to go without – these days it gets demonised as unhealthy, but even if it is who cares? It's the best food in the world!

Brioche Burger Buns

Makes 11 buns

935g Brioche Dough (recipe follows)

1 egg, beaten
salt

15g sesame seeds

Put the dough onto a lightly floured surface and portion into eleven 85g pieces. Form these into balls, and then shape by placing the palm of your hand over a piece of dough and moving it in small concentric circles while applying a light amount of pressure.

Place the shaped dough balls onto a baking tray lined with parchment paper, leaving 4cm between each one. Cover lightly with clingfilm and allow to prove for an additional hour.

Preheat the oven to 180°C. Make an egg wash with the beaten egg and a pinch of salt, then brush it over the tops of the dough balls. Sprinkle them with the sesame seeds.

Bake for 12 minutes, then rotate the tray and bake for approximately 6 minutes more until the buns are golden brown. Cool on a wire rack. These can be stored in an airtight container for 3 days or frozen for 1 month.

Brioche Dough

Makes 935g

500g strong white bread flour
42g sugar
9g salt
7g dry active yeast (or 14g fresh yeast)

255g milk

2 eggs

57g unsalted butter, chilled and diced

Put the flour, sugar, salt and yeast into a stand mixer with the dough hook attachment.

Warm the milk to 35°C and pour it over the dry ingredients, then mix on a medium speed until completely incorporated. Now add the eggs one at time, allowing the first one to be full incorporated before you add the second.

Add the butter a few cubes at a time, making sure they are fully incorporating before adding more. Continue to mix until you have a smooth dough. Place in a well-oiled bowl, cover it with clingfilm and prove for 1 hour (or overnight in the fridge).

Flatbreads

Makes 6 breads

300g strong white bread flour
10g caster sugar
7g dried active yeast
(or 14g fresh yeast)
2g baking powder
5g salt

155g yoghurt
125g warm water

25g butter, melted

80g vegetable oil

Add the flour, sugar, yeast, baking powder and salt to a bowl, then mix in the yoghurt and warm water. Knead until you have a soft dough, then add the melted butter and knead again.

Prove the dough in a bowl covered with clingfilm for 1 hour.

Divide into six 100g balls and roll them out to 2mm thick with a rolling pin. Heat a large frying pan with a little of the oil until it's quite hot. Fry the flatbreads for 2 minutes on each side and cool on a rack.

Focaccia

Makes 1 × 1kg loaf

650g strong white flour
30g coarse polenta
12g dry active yeast
(or 24g fresh yeast)
15g salt
8g olive oil
480g warm water

90g olive oil
6 cloves garlic, thinly sliced
20g rosemary, leaves picked
and chopped fine
10g thyme, leaves picked
sea salt flakes

20 × 20cm baking tin

Place the flour, polenta, yeast and salt in a stand mixer with the dough hook attachment. Turn on to medium speed and add the 8g olive oil and water, then continue to mix for 10 minutes until a stretchy dough forms.

Remove the dough from the mixer and transfer to an oiled bowl. Cover with clingfilm and allow to prove for 60 to 90 minutes, until it doubles in size.

Remove the dough and let it rest for 10 minutes on a well-floured surface. Once it has rested, stretch the dough towards you until it is twice as long, then fold back on itself. Turn it 90°, then repeat the folding/turning process another three times, so you have stretched it four times in all.

Line your baking tin with parchment and spread with 15g of the olive oil. Put the dough in the tin and drizzle with another 30g of olive oil, then knead and push the dough to the edges of the tin. Cover with clingfilm and allow to prove for an additional hour.

Heat the oven to 240°C. Top the proved dough with 15g olive oil, sliced garlic, rosemary, thyme and plenty of sea salt. Place in the oven and immediately reduce the temperature to 190°C. Bake for approximately 25 to 30 minutes, turning once to ensure an even colour.

After baking, drizzle the focaccia with the final 30g of olive oil and allow to cool for about 15 minutes in the tin before turning it out onto a resting rack.

Pain de Mie

Makes 1 × 800g loaf

284g milk
40g water
46g unsalted butter, cubed

440g strong white bread flour
6g dried active yeast (or 12g fresh yeast)
9g sugar
5g salt

900g (21 × 11 × 7cm) loaf tin, greased and lined with parchment paper

Heat the milk, water and butter together, stirring until the butter has melted. Allow to cool to 23°C.

Combine the flour, yeast, sugar and salt in a stand mixer with the dough hook attachment. Mix on a medium speed, slowly adding the cooled milk mixture. Once the liquid is added, increase the speed and mix for 5 minutes more until a firm elastic dough is formed.

Transfer the dough to large, greased bowl, cover with clingfilm and allow to prove until it doubles in size (approximately 1 hour).

Place the dough on a lightly floured service and punch it down. Form into a log shape and place into your prepared bread tin. Lightly cover with clingfilm and allow the dough to prove until it reaches 5cm above the top of the tin (about an hour).

While the bread is proving, preheat the oven to 190°C.

Bake the bread in the bottom third of the oven for 35 minutes. To check if it is properly baked, carefully remove it from the tin and gently knock the base to listen for a hollow sound.

Allow the bread to cool on a rack before slicing.

Soda Bread

Makes 6 mini loaves

200g wholemeal flour
85g plain flour
6g baking powder
10g salt

200g buttermilk
85g stout
50g treacle

30g Rendered Beef Fat (page 233)

20g wheatbran for dusting

6 dariole moulds

It's worth either sourcing decent rendered beef fat from your butcher or making it yourself as it really improves the bread's final flavour.

Preheat the oven to 180°C.

Mix the dry ingredients (the flours, baking powder and salt) together in one bowl and the wet (the buttermilk, stout and treacle) in another.

Melt the rendered beef fat in a small pan. Grease spray the dariole moulds, then weigh 5g of the melted fat into the bottom of each one. Leave to set in the fridge.

Whisk the wet ingredients into the dry until incorporated, then put the mix into a piping bag. Pipe 95g into each mould. Once they're all filled, give the moulds a knock to even out the dough and knock any air out the bottom. Take a palette knife dipped in water and flatten out the top of each one so it's smooth, then cover evenly in bran.

Bake for 10 minutes, using a water spray to generate some steam in the oven. Then turn the temperature down to 170°C and bake for a further 12 minutes.

Once cooked, immediately pop the soda breads out of their tins and cool on a resting rack.

Sourdough

Makes 1 × 900g loaf

475g extra strong bread flour
250g Starter (recipe follows), ideally 3 hours after feeding
12g sea salt

315g water at 23°C

glutinous rice flour for dusting

banneton

At home I usually double everything and make two loaves, then put one in the freezer.

Place the flour, starter and sea salt into a stand mixer with the dough hook attachment. Start to mix on a slow to medium speed, then slowly add the warm water until it is all incorporated. Scrape down the sides if need be and mix for 10 minutes.

Rest the dough, covered with clingfilm or a cool damp cloth, on your work bench for 10 minutes to relax it.

After 10 minutes, stretch and fold the dough. Pick it up in the middle, so either side hangs down, then put it back down so the ends are neatly tucked under and you have a neat-ish ball. Rotate the dough 90° and repeat: do this six times in total.

Rest the dough in a bowl or tub covered in clingfilm or with a lid. After 20 minutes, repeat the six stretch and folds, You need to do this four more times, resting for 20 minutes between each set of stretch and folds.

After your final stretch and fold, lay the dough in a large tray. Clingfilm it, and leave for 6 hours somewhere warm and dry.

Shape the dough into a round ball. Dust your banneton with glutinous rice flour so it lightly coats the entire inside (this will stop the wet dough sticking), and carefully put in the dough ball. Cover loosely and put in the fridge to retard for at least 18 hours and up to 24.

To bake, preheat your oven to 230°C and place a 23cm Dutch oven pot (such as a heavy-duty Le Creuset) in to get hot.

Turn the dough out of the banneton onto a large piece of parchment paper and slash the top, then carefully lower it into the hot pot and put the lid on. Cook for 25 minutes, then take off the lid and cook for another 15 minutes.

Turn the bread out onto a wire rack straight away and rest for a few hours until it's completely cool.

Starter

Day 1

365g milk
150g live kefir

Mix the milk and kefir in a pan and heat to 35°C. Place in a clean bowl and wrap in clingfilm, then leave in a warm, dry place for 24 hours to get the fermentation started.

Day 2

240g strong unbleached bread flour
2L Kilner jar

Whisk the bread flour into the fermented milk/kefir mix. Make sure it is well combined, then put it into the Kilner jar and seal. Leave for 48 hours in a warm, dry place.

Day 4

360g strong unbleached bread flour
200g water or beer
83g milk

Put the starter into a large bowl and whisk in the flour, water or beer and milk.

Make sure it is well combined, then put it back in the Kilner jar and seal. Leave to ferment in a warm, dry place for another 24 hours.

Day 5

Throw away 50% of the starter and leave the remainder in the sealed jar for another 24 hours.

Day 6

300g strong unbleached bread flour
300g water

Put the starter into a large bowl and whisk in the flour and water. Mix thoroughly and return to the jar for a final 24 hours.

Day 7

Your starter is now ready to use. It should be bubbly and nicely acidic.

Storing and Feeding

If you don't want to make bread immediately, keep the starter in the fridge and feed it 3 hours before you plan to begin.

To feed: discard 30% of the starter, then weigh the remainder and mix it with the same quantity of both strong unbleached bread flour and 20°C water.

Good Chef/
Shit Chef

I have always loved chefs' pieces on the rules of being a chef. So, inspired by David Chang's *Eat a Peach* and Daniel Boloud's *Letters to a Young Chef*, and in no particular order, here's my advice to my 18-year-old self.

If the dish pit is a mess, get all your chefs involved in cleaning it; don't walk by it

Have sharp knives, not expensive ones (and learn how to sharpen them)

Be proud of every dish you send; don't send it if it's not right, just do it again

Iron your aprons and uniforms

Get out if you don't like it; life's too fucking short

Travel as much as you can, and eat as many varied cuisines as you can

Drink lots of water, not monster energy drinks

Buy a belt; don't use clingfilm to hold up your trousers

Everything must be labelled and initialled

Say 'good morning' to the chefs and staff each morning

Don't carry spoons in your back pocket near your arse

Don't just stick half-assed prep on the staff shelf for someone else to have to deal with

Be nice to restaurant staff; they have a hard job

Know what to write in sharpies and what to write in ink pen

If you work in hospo and go to other restaurants, don't act like a dick

Don't act like a chef, or how you think a chef should be; be yourself and be genuine

Taste your work a lot

Break down your prep list with times beside it; this way you can race yourself to get done in time

Understand what a good boss actually is: a good boss will care about your career and teach you when needed; a bad boss will exploit you and never do some of the jobs they expect you to do

Put all the morning deliveries away, not just your own items

Maintain a work–life balance as best as possible and see the signs: when you're exhausted, don't go out drinking all night; instead get your rest and eat well

Don't be territorial with clingfilm; everyone needs to use it

Wash out your spoon pots a lot

Don't hoard the nice pans like you own them all

Index

A

A Book of Ideas 6
agar agar 11
Ajo Blanco 180
algae powder 11, 94
Alternative Meats 96, 170
amazake
- Chocolate, Amazake, Salted Milk 112

Anglaise Snow 119
Anster Cheese Espuma 72
Apple Gastrique 172
Aquavit 24
Aquavit restaurant 10, 24
Artichoke Purée 91
Astoria Gyro 33

B

Banh Mi 31
bao bun
- Chicken Bao Buns 152
- Confit Duck Bao Buns 100

Barbados 60, 61
Baron Bigod Custard and Lavosh Crackers 109
Basic Vinaigrette 157, 159, 162, 235
beef
- 50-day Aged Beef, Cherry Mustard, Salsify, Black Garlic 102
- Beef Fat Mayo 143, 233
- Beef Tartar, Black Garlic, Jerusalem Artichoke 143
- My Favourite Cheeseburger 36
- Rendered Beef Fat 233

beetroot
- Beetroot, Smoked Yoghurt, Lanark Blue 159
- Light Pickled Golden Beetroot 161
- Pickled Sliced Beetroot 96, 225
- Roasted Red Beetroot 159
- Salt-baked Beetroot 97

Berkswell Espuma 77
Bibimbap with Bacon and Eggs 195
Black Garlic Condiment 102, 143, 226
Bloomfield, April 46
Blue Ribbon 22
Blueberry Jam 215
Boloud, Daniel 246
Boudin Blanc 200, 202
Braised Salsify 102
Brined Cherries 227
Brined Vegetables 32
brioche
- Brioche Burger Buns 36, 238
- Brioche Dough 100, 152, 238
- Chicken Bao Buns 152
- Confit Duck Bao Buns 100

Broad Bean Ragout 84
Brown Butter Pumpkin 166
Burgers 39
Burnt Apple Ketchup 43, 226
Burrata, Romesco, Red Chilli 146
Bulldog tonkatsu sauce 149, 150
butter 11
- Butter Chicken Curry 204
- Crab Butter 136
- Honey Butter 42

buttermilk fried chicken
- Buttermilk Fried Chicken 41
- Buttermilk Fried Chicken, Tamarind, Coffee 169
- Buttermilk Fried Chicken, Waffles, Honey Butter 41
- Chicken Katsu Sandwich 150

C

Calamansi Gel 115
Candied Walnuts 122
Caramelised Onions 39
Carlsberg 18
carrot
- Brined Vegetables 32
- Carrot Purée 123
- Carrot Salad 196

cast iron pans 14
celeriac
- Celeriac Tart Shell 67
- Celeriac Tartlet, Sea Trout, Sour Cream, Sea Buckthorn 66

Cep Purée 76
chaat masala 205
Chang, David 246
Channel Wrack 167
Chantilly Cream 212
Char Sui Chicken 32
chawanmushi
- Truffle Chawanmushi 76

cheese:
- Anster Cheese Espuma 72
- Baron Bigod Custard 109
- Berkswell Espuma 77
- Burrata, Romesco, Red Chilli 146
- Cheddar Custard 158
- Gnudi, Spring Vegetables and Lemon Butter Sauce 46
- Hogget, Peas, Nori, Ewe's Curds
- My Favourite Cheeseburger 36
- Parmesan Consommé 79
- Parmesan Pastry shell 189
- Sheep's Milk Agnolotti 80
- Squash, Pear, Goat's Curds, Kinako Dressing 162
- Tomato Salad 183

Cherry Mustard 102, 227
chicken
- Banh Mi 31
- Butter Chicken Curry 204
- Buttermilk Fried Chicken 41
- Buttermilk Fried Chicken, Tamarind, Coffee 169
- Buttermilk Fried Chicken, Waffles, Honey Butter 41
- Char Sui Chicken 32

chicken (*cont.*)
Chicken Bao Buns 152
Chicken Katsu Sandwich 150
Chicken Sauce 52
Chicken Souvlaki 34
Chicken Tikka 205
Confit Chicken Balls 152
Confit Chicken Leg 153
Crispy Chicken Skin 153
Roast Chicken 50
Roast Chicken Stock 44, 52, 82, 203
chocolate
Chocolate, Amazake, Salted Milk 112
Chocolate, Miso, Hazelnut 173
Chocolate Mousse 173
Chocolate Mousse with Miso Crème Centre 114
Chocolate Tart 212
Chocolate Tuille 115
Miso Chocolate Fudge 218
White Chocolate Spray 114
Coffee Gastrique 169
compote
Rhubarb Compote 118
Tamarind Compote 170, 227
Yellow Tomato Compote 183
confit
Confit Chicken Balls 152
Confit Chicken Leg 153
Confit Duck Bao Buns 100
Connaught, The 20
Cooking Liquid (for boudin blanc) 203
Corner Bistro 36
Corrigan, Richard 66
Crab Butter 136
crackers
Lavosh Crackers 111
Linseed Crackers 161
cream
Chantilly Cream 212
Vanilla Cream 215
Crispy Chicken Skin 153
croustade
Croustade 71
croustade iron 14
Croutons 77
cucumber
Compressed Cucumber 90, 223
Compressed Cucumber and Kohlrabi 138, 223
Cucumber and Yoghurt Chutney 33, 205
cured fish
Cured Halibut 82
Cured Trout, Ponzu, Cucumber, Kohlrabi 138
Cured Trout 138
Cured Turbot 90
Sea Trout Tartar 67
custard
Anglaise Snow 119
Baron Bigod Custard 109
Cheddar Custard 158
Custard Tart 208

D

deggi mirch 205
dehydrator 14
dill
Dill Emulsion 90, 231
Dill Oil 136, 138, 164, 231
Doughnuts 214
Ducasse, Alain 102
duck
Duck Breast, Umeboshi, Beetroot, Chicory 96
Confit Duck 100
Confit Duck Balls 100
Confit Duck Bao Buns 100
Goosnargh Duck 96
Dufresne, Wylie 41

E

Eat a Peach 246
Edible Razor Clam Shells 94
eggs 11
Anglaise Snow 119
Baron Bigod Custard 109
Bibimbap with Bacon and Eggs 194
Cheddar Custard 158
Custard Tart 208
Egg Yolk Emulsion 232
Elderflower Sabayon 84
Prosciutto and Tomato Herb Tart 188
Swiss Meringue 175
Truffle Chawanmushi 76
Vanilla Cream 214
Elderflower Sabayon 84
emulsion
Dill Emulsion 90, 231
Egg Yolk Emulsion 232
Herb Emulsion 104, 232
Lovage Emulsion 138, 232
Mustard Emulsion 43, 232
Errington Farm 159
espuma
Anster Cheese Espuma 72
Berkswell Espuma 77

F

Fahy, Ash 212
Fermented Tomato
Fermented Tomato Gel 89
Fermented Tomato Water 89
Ferguson, Neil 50
Fife 71
fish
Celeriac Tartlet, Sea Trout, Sour Cream, Sea Buckthorn 66
Cured Trout, Ponzu, Cucumber, Kohlrabi 138
Exmoor caviar 41, 90
Wild Halibut, Summer Vegetables, Elderflower 82
Wild Turbot, Razor Clams, Pickled Cucumber, Sauce Vin Blanc, Exmoor Caviar 90
Flatbreads 33, 204, 239
Focaccia 239
fondant 11
Foolproof Rice 205
Frantzen, Bjorn 66
French Laundry Cookbook, The 10
Furikake 134

G

Gala Pie 184
gastrique
Apple Gastrique 172
Coffee Gastrique 169
Red Wine Gastrique 97
gel
Calamansi Gel 115
Fermented Tomato Gel 89
Ponzu Gel 67
Tomato Ponzu Fluid Gel 140
gelatine 11
Geranium 90
Glenrothes 8
Glocker, Markus 43, 221
glucose 11
Gnudi 47
Gnudi, Spring Vegetables and Lemon Butter Sauce 46
Goosnargh duck 96
Graham Cracker Crust 56
gram scale 14

Granola 111
Great British Menu 66, 86, 104
Gullane 120

H

Hagi 192
hand blender 14
herb
Herb Emulsion 104, 232
Herb Oil 231
Prosciutto and Tomato Herb Tart 188
hogget
Hogget, Peas, Nori, Ewe's Curds 104
Hogget Sauce 105
Honey Butter 42
Hummus 34

I

Iberico Presa, Nahm Jim, Apple 170
ice cream
Salted Milk 115
Ice Cream Sandwich 54
invert sugar 11
iSi siphon gun 14
Isle of Wight tomatoes 183
isomalt 11
Isolmalt Tuille 122

J

Jade Johnston 127, 146, 179
jam, blueberry 215
Japanese mandolin 14
Jersualem artichoke
Artichoke Purée 91
Beef Tartar, Black Garlic, Jerusalem Artichoke 143
Jerusalem Artichoke, Cheddar, Maple 157
Jerusalem Artichoke Shells 157
J-choke Chips 145

K

Kamozawa, Aki 6
Kataifi Nests 115
katsu
Chicken Katsu Sandwich 150
Keller, Thomas 10
Kewpie Mayo 31, 149, 150, 233
kilner jars 15
Kimchi 150, 192, 195
Kinako Dressing 162, 235
Kohlrabi Purée 89
Kombucha 64
Krystal 17, 33, 60, 61, 62, 127, 192

L

lamb
Hogget, Peas, Nori, Ewe's Curds 104
Lavosh Crackers 111
Letters to a Young Chef 246
Linseed Cracker 161
liquid nitrogen 15
lobster
Lobster Knuckle-stuffed Onions 88
Lobster, Kohlrabi, Yoghurt 86
Lobster Sauce 88
Lobster Tails 86
London NYC, the 20, 50
Lovage Emulsion 138, 232
Lovage Oil 231

M

Malted Barley Semifreddo 56
Maple Glaze 158
mayo
Beef Fat Mayo 233
Kewpie Mayo 31, 149, 150, 233
Miso Mustard Mayo 132, 235
Onion Mayo 152, 234
Tamarind Mayo 169
microplane 15
miso
Miso Caramel 175
Miso Chocolate Fudge 219
Miso Crème 114
Miso Mustard Mayo 132, 235
Modernist Cuisine 102
moulds 15
mousse
Chocolate Mousse 173
Chocolate Mousse with Miso Crème Centre 114
mushrooms:
Cep Purée 76
Mushroom Leaf Crisps 77
Pickled Shimeji Mushrooms 143, 222
Roasted Mushrooms 76
Shiitake and Beansprout Salad 197
Truffle Chawanmushi 76
mustard
Cherry Mustard 102
Miso Mustard Mayo 235
Mustard Emulsion 43
Pickled Mustard Seeds 222
My Favourite Cheeseburger 36

N

Nahm Jim 172
Newlyn 8, 214
Norinade 105, 108
Noto, Bob 125, 130, 131

O

oil
Dill Oil 136, 138, 164
Herb Oil 231
Lovage Oil 231
onion
Caramelised Onions 39
Onion Croustade 71
Onion Fondue 72
Onion Mayo 152, 234
Onion Purée 234
Onion Rings 166
Onion Salt 100, 153
Pickled Silverskin Onions 232
oven temperatures 15

P

Pain de Mie 149, 150, 240
Pak Choi 197
Parker Meridian 36
Parmesan
Parmesan Consommé 79
Parmesan Pastry Shell 189
pasta
Sheep's Milk Agnolotti, Parmesan Consommé 79
Pasta Dough 80
pasta machine 15
Pastrami Spice 44
Pastry 185
Edible Razor Clam Shells 94
Kataifi Nests 115
Parmesan Pastry Shell 189
Sweet Tart Shell 209

Pâté en Croûte 184
Pea Tart 108
Picked Crabmeat 136
Pickle Liquor 222
  Pickled Lettuce 104, 223
  Pickled Mustard Seeds 43, 222
  Pickled Shallot Rings 159, 222
  Pickled Shimeji Mushrooms 143, 222
  Pickled Radicchio 102, 225
  Pickled Red Chicory 96, 225
  Pickled Silverskin Onions 43, 223
  Pickled Sliced Beetroot 96, 225
  Pickled Wild Leek Buds 71, 225
  Pickled Wild Leeks 79, 223
Pizza 26
  Pizza Dough 28
  pizza oven 15
plastic piping bags 15
pomace oil 12
ponzu
  Ponzu Base 140
  Ponzu Gel 66
  Tomato Ponzu Fluid Gel 140
pork
  Bibimbap with Bacon and Eggs 194
  Boudin Blanc 202
  Iberico Presa, Nahm Jim, Apple 170
  Pâté en Croute 185
  Pork Belly with Bulgogi Sauce 196
  Tête de Cochon Terrine 43
posset
  Sea Buckthorn Posset 122
potato
  Potato Dauphine 134
  Potato Dauphine, Miso Mustard Mayo 132
  Potato Mousseline 203
  Puffed Potato 134
prawn
  Prawn Paste 149
  Prawn Toast 149
  Quick XO Sauce 198
Prosciutto and Tomato Herb Tart 188
Prune Gravy 203
pumpkin
  Brown Butter Pumpkin 166
  Scallops, Pumpkin, Yuzu Kosho 164
purée
  Artichoke Purée 91
  Carrot Purée 123
  Cep Purée 76
  Kohlrabi Purée 89
  Onion Purée 234
  Rhubarb Purée 118, 119
  Sweetcorn Purée 51
  Umeboshi Purée 96, 227
Pyrus Botanicals 73

Q

Queens 33
Quick XO Sauce 198

R

Ramsay, Gordon 17, 20, 22, 31, 43, 79, 164
razor clam
  Edible Razor Clam Shells 94
  Razor Clam Tartar 94
Red Wine Gastrique 97
Reduction 167
Rendered Beef Fat 233, 241
rhubarb
  Rhubarb and Custard 117
  Rhubarb Compote 118
  Rhubarb Glass 119
  Rhubarb Purée 118, 119
  Rhubarb Sorbet 118
Ricotta Filling (for agnolotti) 80
Roast Cherry Tomatoes 188
Roast Chicken and Sweetcorn Succotash 50
Roast Squash 162
Roasted Mushrooms 76
Roasted Red Beetroot 159
Roberta's 26
Robuchon, Joël 10
Romesco 146

S

Saigon Bakery 31
salad:
  Beetroot, Smoked Yoghurt, Lanark Blue 159
  Carrot Salad 196
  Pak Choi 197
  Shiitake and Beansprout Salad 197
  Squash, Pear, Goat's Curds, Kinako Dressing 162
  Tomato Salad 182
salsify
  Braised Salsify 102
Salt-baked Beetroot 97
Salted Milk Ice Cream 115
Samuelsson, Marcus 10, 24
Sandy Lane 60, 61, 204, 208
sauce:
  Chicken Sauce 52
  Elderflower Sabayon 84
  Hogget Sauce 105
  Lemon Butter Sauce 46
  Lobster Sauce 88
  Prune Gravy 203
  Quick XO Sauce 198
  Romesco 146
  San Marzano Tomato Sauce 28
  Sauce Vin Blanc 91
  Watercress Sauce 84
San Marzano Tomato Sauce 28
Scallops, Pumpkin, Yuzu Kosho 164
Sea Buckthorn
  Celeriac Tartlet, Sea Trout, Sour Cream, Sea Buckthorn 66
  Sea Buckthorn Posset, Yoghurt, Carrot, Walnut 120
  sea salt 11
sea trout
  Cured Trout 138
  Sea Trout Tartar 67
Sheep's Milk Agnolotti 80
  Sheep's Milk Agnolotti, Parmesan Consommé 79
Sherry Vinegar Jelly 77
Shiitake and Beansprout Salad 197
Smoked Yoghurt 161
smoker gun 15
Soda Bread 241
sorbet
  Rhubarb Sorbet 118
  Yoghurt Sorbet 123
Sour Cream Dome 67
Sourdough 244
  Sourdough Starter 245
soy lecithin 12
Spicy Sugar 215
spiraliser 15
Spotted Pig 46
Spring Vegetables 47
squash
  Roast Squash 162
  Squash, Pear, Goat's Curds, Kinako Dressing 162
staff tea 177, 195
steamer 15
stock
  Roast Chicken Stock 44, 52, 82, 203
Sweet Tart Shell 209
sweetcorn

Sweetcorn Purée 51
Sweetcorn Succotash 51
Swiss Meringue 175

T

Talbot, Alex 6
Tamarind Compote 170, 227
Tamarind Mayo 169, 234
tart
Celeriac Tartlet, Sea Trout, Sour Cream, Sea Buckthorn 66
Chocolate Tart 212
Custard Tart 208
Pea Tart 108
Prosciutto and Tomato Herb Tart
tartar
Beef Tartar 145
Razor Clam Tartar 94
Tête de Cochon Terrine 43
Tête de Cochon 44
thermometers 15
Thermomix 15
Toasted Hazelnuts 175
tomato
Fermented Tomato Gel 89
Fermented Tomato Water 89
Roast Cherry Tomatoes 189
San Marzano Tomato Sauce 28
Tomato Ponzu Fluid Gel 140
Tomato Salad 183
Tomato Stall, The 182
trisol 12
Trotter, Charlie 10
trout
Cured Trout 138
Sea Trout Tartar 66
Truffle Chawanmushi 76
Truffle Chawanmushi, Mushrooms, Berkswell Cheese 73
tuillle
Chocolate Tuille 115
Isomalt Tuille 122

U

Umeboshi Purée 96, 226
ultratex 12

V

Vanilla Cream 215
vegetable oil 12
vegetables
Braised Salsify 102
Brined Vegetables 32
Broad Bean Ragout 84
Brown Butter Pumpkin 166
Salt-baked Beetroot 97
Spring Vegetables 47
Sweetcorn Succotash 51
vinaigrette
Basic Vinaigrette 157, 159, 162, 235
White Balsamic Vinaigrette 183, 235
vinegars 12

W

Waffles 42
walnuts
Candied Walnuts 122
Watercress Sauce 84
WD-50 41
White Balsamic Vinaigrette 183, 235
White Chocolate Spray 114
Wild Garlic Pesto 81
Wild Halibut, Summer Vegetables, Elderflower 82
Wild Turbot, Razor Clams, Pickled Cucumber, Sauce Vin Blanc, Exmoor Caviar 90

X

xanthan gum 12
XO Fried Rice 198

Y

yeast 12
Yellow Tomato Compote 183
Yoghurt Sorbet 123
Yuzu Kosho Beurre Blanc 167

Acknowledgements

At the risk of sounding like a cringey Oscar speech, I do have a lot of people to thank…

My publishers, Emily and Nasim, for all their help and advice and without whose expertise the book would not have come together. Clare Skeats, who designed the book and really understood the brief.

Clair Irwin, for the amazing photographs and for being cool to work with.

My PR company, Soundbite, for making the introduction to Kitchen Press and getting the whole project going.

Krystal, for the tons of work she did on the book, the constant reading and rereading and for generally supporting me in the process. Thanks for all the work you do in our life together, and a special thanks to my amazing boys, Sonny and Jesse xxx

Jade Johnston, who runs the restaurants alongside me, for all the advice and support along the way and for continuing to believe in the vision of the companies and trusting me x

All the teams at Aizle and Noto, both back and front of house, and to the chefs for their help and patience on the book-shoot days: in particular Lewis for organising Aizle's shoots and helping with all the styling, and Alberto for managing the Noto shoot. Thanks to Rachel and Rosie for working the extra days.

A big shout-out to Ash Fahy, one of my longest-serving sous chefs, who helped tons with the writing and formatting and who went through the back catalogues to find the old recipes, #cantstopwontstop.

A big shout out to my blood: Mum, Gary dog and my brothers Scott and Calum who always back me, no matter what.

My friends and chef mentors, Ian McNaught and David Williams, for all the memories and advice and for inspiring me to be the best I can be and not to give up.

Christina, for being my oldest friend and for being there and supporting the sites when I needed it, and for floating me money to cover VAT payments in between expansions.

Fraz Smith, my good friend for lots of years, thanks mate, five-a-side master and good drinking friend lol.

Brian Grigor, a true friend and one of the most dedicated and professional chefs I have ever known, for the continued belief and friendship. Thank you for Averie.

Chris Graham, baddest man on the planet xx

Stuart and Frances Collins of Dockett No. 33, amazing friends. Thanks for all you've done for me, from feeding me when I was broke, Stuart, to giving us tables for Noto to open. I'll never forget your generosity and friendship.

To the teams past and present of Aizle, Noto and Tipo, and anyone who's played a part in the successes and the hard work in the early years: Mark Love, Big Stu, Matt Smith (wee mental Davie).

My Ditmars boys: Chris Abbamondi, Ken "man of steel" Corrow and Rob Rubba for the early days in NYC x

Chefs who've inspired me along the way, some I've worked with, some I've met, some I've staged with and some I've never met but all have had a profound influence on me….

Gordon Ramsay, Neil Ferguson (for even giving me the chance to work with you), Josh Emmet, Markus Glocker (for still being a legend, thank you) and to all the cooks I worked with in NYC – there are too many to name but I remember everyone and appreciate all of those moments.

Chefs like David Chang, Wylie Dufresne, Simon Rogan, who I try to emulate in my own way.

Lastly, to all the guests who've come to our restaurants and who continue to come, thank you for believing in us, supporting us and trusting us to deliver x

Noto's iPad
Noto's iPad

First published in the UK in 2023 by
Kitchen Press Ltd,
1 Windsor Place,
Dundee, DD2 1BG

www.kitchenpress.co.uk

Notebook photography by Rebecca Milling at Copystand
www.copystand.co.uk

Designed by Clare Skeats

ISBN 9781739174019

A CIP catalogue record for the book is available from the British Library

Printed in India

- Pear gnocchi with brown butter and lemon zest
- Lobster and roast lemon sauce.
- Squid ink spatzle.
- Parsnip & horseradish puree.
- Escargot ravioli with garlic soup and oyster tempura
- Fish tartare with Tequila jelly.
- Hot ice cubes and methocel, gellan gum.
- Chocolate & ginger souffle?
- Truffled carrot puree.
- Saffron stewed fennel shavings.
- Apple Cappuccino, with chestnut biscotti and Cinnamon froth.
- Grand Marnier/Mascarpone filled chocolate agnolotti.
- Figs with Jack daniels.
- Duck dry rubbed Mace / blueberries Smoked?
- Green tea / Pineapple / cloves or anise.
- Green tea Curry dust for fish.
- Caramelised peanut ice/cream.
- Roasted Fruits with Juniper Ice-Cream.
- Pesto ice-cream.
- Tea Smoked Quail with dried cherry Puree.

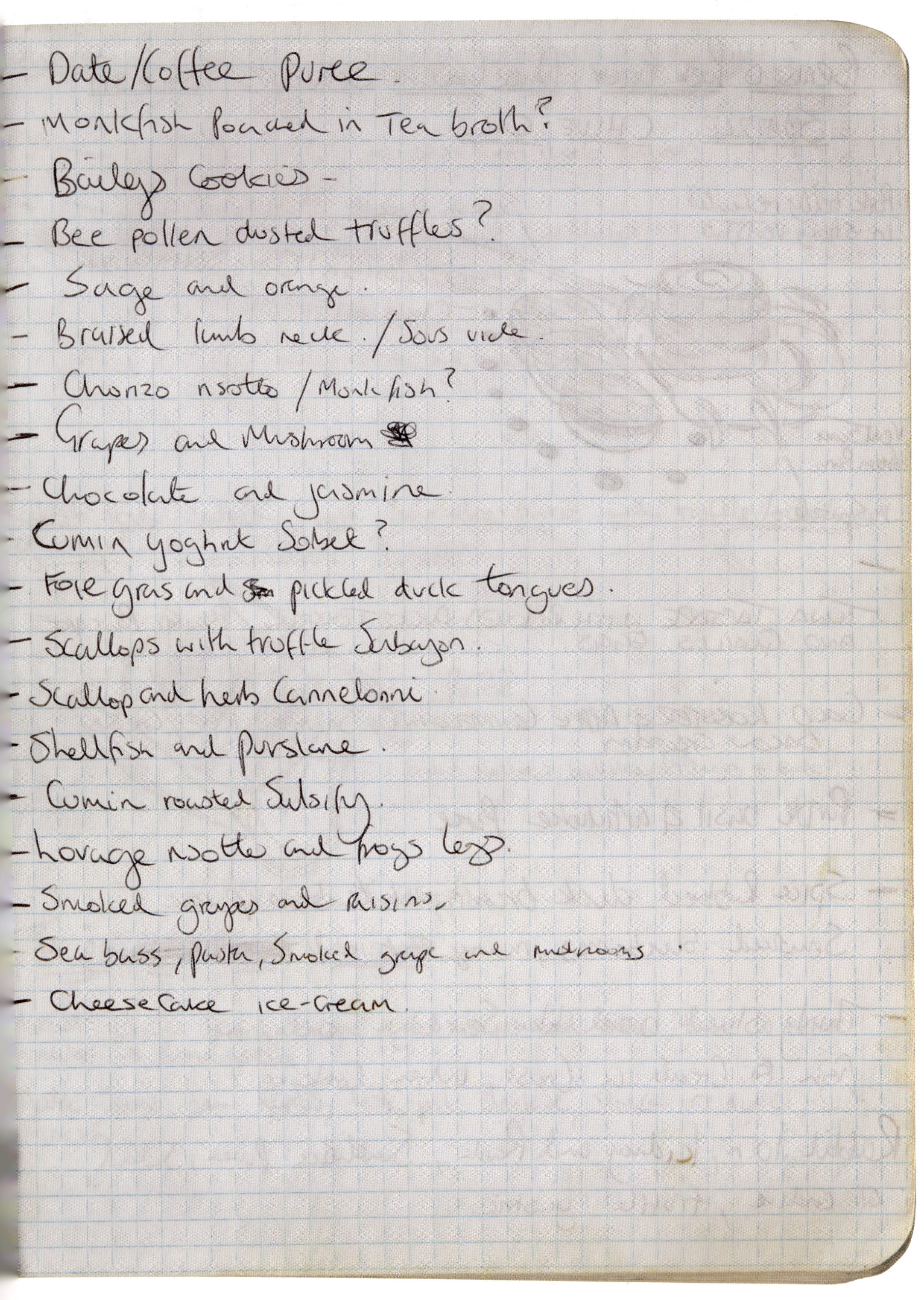

- Date/Coffee Puree.
- Monkfish poached in Tea broth?
- Baileys Cookies -
- Bee pollen dusted truffles?
- Sage and orange.
- Braised lamb neck./Sous vide.
- Chorizo risotto/Monkfish?
- Grapes and Mushroom
- Chocolate and jasmine.
- Cumin yoghurt Sorbet?
- Foie gras and pickled duck tongues.
- Scallops with truffle Sabayon.
- Scallop and herb Cannelonni.
- Shellfish and purslane.
- Cumin roasted Salsify.
- Lovage risotto and frogs legs.
- Smoked grapes and raisins,
- Sea bass, pasta, Smoked grape and mushrooms.
- Cheesecake ice-cream.